Hear My Voice

Hear My Voice

Tales of Trauma and Equity from Today's Youth

Edited by Heather Dean
and Amber E. Wagnon

ROWMAN & LITTLEFIELD
Lanham • Boulder • New York • London

Published by Rowman & Littlefield
An imprint of The Rowman & Littlefield Publishing Group, Inc.
4501 Forbes Boulevard, Suite 200, Lanham, Maryland 20706
www.rowman.com

6 Tinworth Street, London SE11 5AL, United Kingdom

British Library Cataloguing in Publication Information Available

Library of Congress Cataloging-in-Publication Data
ISBN 9781475853346 (cloth : alk. paper)
ISBN 9781475853353 (pbk. : alk. paper)
ISBN 9781475853360 (electronic)

To all the students who walked through my classroom doors and taught me how to be a better teacher, this book is for you.

To all the teacher education candidates who regularly inspire me with their commitment to students and who continue to help me learn about the individual in my classroom, regardless of their age, this book is for you.

For my husband, who never wavers in his support and belief in me, this book is for you.

For my children, who taught me so much more than I could ever teach them and through the opportunity to parent them, I learned to be a better teacher, this book is for you.

With love,

Mrs. Dean/Dr. Dean/Heather/Mom

To each of my students, past and present, thank you for the lessons you imparted upon me.

To each teacher candidate I have had the opportunity to work alongside, thank you for motivating me to continue to learn. It is my hope that this book will assist you on your journey as an educator.

To my husband, thank you for always believing in me.

To my children, you will always be my greatest accomplishments. Thank you for the daily inspiration!

To my childhood friend, Leann. Your life, though short, will always be my inspiration to bring empathy and kindness into the world.

Mrs. Wagnon/Dr. Wagnon/Mom/Amber

Contents

Preface

In the 1993–1994 school year, Professor of Education Renate Nummela Caine and her husband, Geoffrey Cain, embarked on a three-year study examining the integration of brain-based instruction in an elementary school. It was one of the first studies of its kind. Their goal at Dry Creek Elementary was "to change assumptions about schools, learning, and teaching; to encourage teachers' own efforts to implement brain-based instruction" (Caine & Caine, 1995).

Brain-based instruction/education is based on the cognitive and constructive models of learning, which have been studied for over thirty years by physiological researchers (Bruer, 2008). These important research endeavors have enabled educators to examine, evaluate, and understand teaching and learning.

However, the gaps in such research are evident when brain functions in regard to learning are considered (Bruer, 2008). In fact, Bruer (2008) argues that "for nearly a century, the science of the mind (psychology) developed independently from the science of the brain (neuroscience) (p. 52). However, recent advances in "neuroimaging has enabled scientists to study the human brain at work in vivo, deepening our understanding of the very complex processes underpinning speech and language, thinking and reasoning, reading and mathematics" (Goswami, 2008, p. 4). A collaboration between neuroscience and education continues to emerge globally.

Usha Goswami, professor of cognitive development and director of the Centre for Neuroscience in Education at St. John's College in Cambridge, explains that neuroscience "investigates the processes by which the brain learns and remembers, from the molecular and cellular levels right through to brain systems" and encompasses neurology, psychology, and biology (2008, p. 33). Professor Goswami further asserts that there are over 100 billion neurons in a human brain that connect to other neurons and the connectivity of neurons "are thoughts to correspond to particular mental states or mental representations" (200, p. 34). Learning occurs when changes in connectivity occur, thus meaning that teaching, in part, influences brain function by facilitating changes in connectivity (Goswami, 2008).

Through these new advances we are seeing some shifts in the way educators approach students. For example, a *Washington Post* article details how St. Andrew's Episcopal School in Potomac is working with Johns Hopkins University School of Education to utilize brain-based research across their school in instructional methods (Strauss, 2013).

We recognize that changes are difficult to activate in the standardized educational system many educators find themselves confined to. In this text we use the word "educators" to include all educational stakeholders, including classroom teachers, counselors, diagnosticians, administrators, social workers, and other educational staff. Our text also moves past teaching and learning, to examine how brain-based research can inform educators' ability to reach the whole student, including their socio-emotional needs. It is our hope that *Hear My Voice: Tales of Trauma and Equity from Today's Youth*, and the student narratives within, will enable our readers to establish a pathway in which brain-based research can impact their work with students.

REFERENCES

Bruer, J. T. (2008). In search of brain-based education. In M. H. Immordino-Yang & K. Fischer (Eds.), *The Jossey-Bass reader on the brain and learning* (pp. 51–69). San Francisco, CA: Josey-Bass.

Caine, R., & G. Caine. (1994). *Making connections: Teaching and the human brain.* Menlo Park, CA: Addison-Wesley.

Caine, R. N., & G. Caine (1995). Reinventing schools through brain-based learning. *Educational Leadership, 52*(7), 43–47.

Goswami, U. (2008). Neuroscience and education. In M. H. Immordino-Yang & K. Fischer (Eds.), *The Jossey-Bass reader on the brain and learning* (pp. 33–50). San Francisco, CA: Josey-Bass.

Strauss, V. (2013, March 5). A school brings brain research to the center of its curriculum. *The Washington Post.* Retrieved from https://www.washingtonpost.com/

Acknowledgments

We would like to thank those that bravely shared their narratives with us so that we could learn from them.* We thank you for your generosity and bravery in sharing your story. We know that your story will have an impact on many that work with children! Thank you!

With much appreciation,

Heather Dean and *Amber E. Wagnon*

NOTE

* All narratives included within this book represent the experiences of one individual and are in no way meant to represent any group as a whole. Additionally, pseudonyms have been used to allow for the confidentiality of all those who shared their stories.

Introduction

Heather Dean, PhD, and Amber E. Wagnon, PhD

We cannot educate a child we do not know. We cannot educate a child we do not love. Consequently, a child will not want to learn from someone that does not know them or love them.

When we left our secondary positions as English teachers, we left with a great love for our students, our profession, and our colleagues and with a desire to teach the next generation of educators. Spending time with groups of preservice teachers has brought us both joy and renewed confidence for our profession. Time and time again, young teacher candidates tell us they dreamed of being a teacher as a child. With eyes lit up, they share about the difference they want to make and the ways they hope to connect to today's students. This is a great example of the passion all of us need to keep in this profession.

While education is an exhausting and, at times, a thankless job, we must stay connected to what stirred us to this profession in the first place. We truly believe teachers enter this field from a place of genuine care and love for both the students and their content.

If you learn and are inspired like us, it is the personal story that reminds you why you are important and why you matter to the lives in your room. This book was compiled with that hope in mind and also with you in mind. We know your plate is full. We know the to-do list is longer than the list of unclaimed minutes in your day. From a teacher's heart, we hope these stories remind you of how much your unique talents and gifts are needed by the students sitting in your classroom this year. Their lives are often complicated and messy. As you read the following narratives, please be reminded of your purpose. Enjoy the journey!

We would love to hear from you. Please share your stories and your journey with us at https://educatorsinpursuit.com/.

All the best,

Heather and Amber

Chapter 1

Identity Interrupted: A Student in Foster Care

Donald M. Hume, PhD

To be yourself in a world that is constantly trying to make you something else is the greatest accomplishment.

Ralph Waldo Emerson

Expected Chapter Learning Outcomes:

- Readers will gain insight into the experiences of a high school student with a tumultuous home environment that leads to intake into the foster system.
- Readers will be provided with research that connects to experiences of the student highlighted in this chapter.
- Readers will develop approaches to help students navigate the complex emotional and academic challenges they face.

It is easy to assume that everyone's experience in life has been similar to one's own. Many of us come from backgrounds that include at least one parent who has been a constant presence in our lives, directing us when we are young and leading us to discover our own personalities as we grow older.

Teachers are expected to provide meaningful lessons on myriad subjects to a diverse group of students every day. Often our training on diversity focuses on students with needs that are clearly identifiable through external signals: English-language learners and students with Individualized Educational Plans (IEPs). However, some students bring needs with them that can be more difficult to identify and support.

Let's look at an example of a student who has been removed from the only home he has ever known. What needs would a student in this situation have in a classroom? How would you recognize these needs? What external signals might such a student display? How might a student's sense that he has lost his own identity manifest itself in a classroom?

STUDENT NARRATIVE

Matt: A Student in Foster Care

They say you don't know what you have until you miss it. I never thought much about whether my life growing up was a stable environment or not. Looking back, I realize there wasn't much structure in our daily lives. My older twin sisters began their rebellious phases pretty early in their lives, and my mother was often out working one of her two jobs so she could provide for us. My sisters had known our father, but, a few days after I was born, he and my mother had a mean argument. He left that night, and no one heard from him again for years.

By the time they were in the sixth grade, my sisters had both been suspended from school for using drugs. My mother tried to get them involved in sports, but with her two jobs she didn't have time to take them to practices or games herself. My sisters made friends playing softball, though, so it wasn't long before they were spending most of their time after school out of the house, either at practice or hanging out with friends. That left me alone most of the time after school, even though I was only 8 years old.

What my mother didn't realize was that my sisters used softball as an alternative place to party. It was much easier for them to hang out with friends and smoke when all the adults figured they were practicing. They stayed out of trouble at school that way, but their habits evolved from inhaling whipped-cream aerosols and fingernail polish remover, to smoking weed (what they were suspended for), eventually to taking hydros (hydrocodone tablets).

Hydros were easy for them because they didn't smell like the other drugs they had tried. Add a little vodka in a sports bottle and they were set for the day. Their teammates would join them when they partied on weekends, but my sisters were usually high every day.

At first, I didn't know what was going on, since they were so much older than I was, in the seventh grade while I was in second. I knew that I was home alone a lot more than my other second-grade friends, but that was just the way things had always been; it didn't seem unusual to me. By the time I was eleven, though, I knew a lot more than my mother did about what my sisters were hiding in the back of their desk drawers.

My life seemed normal to me. My sisters would wake me up in the morning after my mother had left for work. I'd have a bowl of cereal and get dressed for school. I would walk to my elementary school; my sisters would get picked up by their friends to drive across town to the high school. After school, I would walk home and spend the afternoon alone, watching TV or making myself a snack if there was any food in the fridge. I'd usually see my mom in the evening a few nights a week when she didn't get hours at her second job, but often I was by myself until my sisters got home after nine.

It was the end of my seventh-grade year when everything changed. My grades had never been very good, but they never mattered much to me. Mrs. Knox was the first teacher who ever got angry with me for not doing my work. I really didn't like her. She had started talking about holding me back if my grades didn't improve and insisted that my mother come in for a conference. I tried to explain that my mother wasn't available, but that just made Mrs. Knox angrier. I didn't want to be held back and have my friends all think there was something wrong with me. On the way home that afternoon, I made a decision.

I don't think I was really trying to kill myself. I didn't know how strong the hydros were, or how many to take. I don't actually remember taking them, but I woke up in the hospital with a tube up my nose and a police officer standing behind my mother. After that, I woke up alone in what I later found out was the psych ward on a seventy-two-hour hold. They spent a lot of time asking me why I tried to kill myself, and I just remember being confused about why they were asking me that.

It was shortly after I got out of the hospital that I found out that my father, whom I had never met, had decided that my mother wasn't taking care of me and applied to the court to take me away from her. I was angry that someone I didn't even know was judging me and my family. He didn't want my sisters, just me.

The day we went to court I wore a button-up shirt and a tie my mother had borrowed from a neighbor. The judge decided that he wasn't sure I should go with my father, but that I should definitely not go home with my mother. I was whisked out of the courtroom and downstairs to a holding room with a few other kids. We were loaded into a white van with a large Sherriff's badge pasted on the side. I remember thinking we were being sent to jail. Of course, we weren't, but to me there wasn't much difference.

Arriving at Cherry Hill Children's Home wasn't much different than arriving at jail. The van went through a gate in high walls to an enclosed court-yard, where we were unloaded and seated in folding chairs in a bare white waiting room. We were called one by one into a smaller room where we were processed in. I arrived with nothing but the clothes I wore to court. I wasn't allowed to go home to get clothes or any of my belongings. They tried to be friendly, but I was confused and just wanted to go home. They asked if I had any weapons or drugs on me, and I had to empty my pockets onto the table.

From the processing room I was taken to what amounted to a large closet, filled with clothes that weren't mine. I was instructed to pick out something to *wear now and something for the next day. Then I was brought to a bedroom that had three futons in it that I was to share with two other boys about my age and left alone with them.*

You'd think I would be used to being alone, but this was different. When I was in my own house and alone, I understood the situation. My possessions were all nearby, and I could go outside to meet a friend, or go to my room to play a video game or watch what I wanted on TV. Here, nothing was mine.

There was a common room with a TV, but it usually was set to some educational cartoon for the much younger kids. They wouldn't let us change the channel to anything that might be more interesting for us older kids because it might have something deemed "inappropriate." The bed wasn't mine. The clothes weren't mine. Nothing was mine. I couldn't even decide when or what to eat. There was nothing to do but wait and hope you could go home.

But I couldn't. I found out three days later that I was going to be sent to live with a foster family. These were people I didn't know, in a neighborhood I didn't know. Luckily school had just gotten out for the summer, but in the fall I'd be attending a new school near where this foster family lived. I wouldn't see anyone I knew from my old school ever again.

When the Miller family came to pick me up from Cherry Hill, they looked like a family from a Macy's catalog. Their home was not so welcoming, though. There were two of us from Cherry Hill assigned to this couple. We shared a bedroom where we were locked in at night. We could only eat during mealtimes. There was a padlock on the refrigerator. We were allowed to make no decisions for ourselves. That was a very boring few months.

Once school started, I made no effort to get to know anyone. This wasn't my school. I wasn't planning on staying here, so I didn't care at all about learning anything. The teachers didn't seem to care, either. I remember it was the week before Halloween when I was allowed to go home with my mother again. I was so happy to be back in my own room with my own clothes again. I still didn't see my mother much. She was working two jobs at that point, and one of my sisters had just been arrested and sent to Juvenile Hall for selling hydros at school. It was a bad week for my mom, and in all that stress, she forgot to re-enroll me in my old school.

The police came to pick me up when I was home alone the next week. They took me back to Cherry Hill where I stayed for another three days until I was sent to another foster family. They were more pleasant than my first placement, and I was the only kid in the house. I spent the rest of eighth grade with them. They moved out of state the following summer, however, so I was back in Cherry Hill for most of that summer.

Starting high school, I was placed with my third foster family. It happened to be the family of a classmate of mine from third grade. We hadn't been friends, but we knew of each other. Their house had a lot of rules I hadn't had before, such as a strict curfew of 9 pm. They also required us to eat dinner together every night, and I had to take a drug test every week. I was not happy about these rules, especially since they seemed to apply to me much more than to their own son (who never had to take a drug test). I broke them often.

Their son had joined the high school surf team and had to be at the beach each morning at 6:30 am. This meant that, whether I wanted to or not, I had to also join the surf team. They would drive us together in the morning and didn't want to have to drive me separately to school. I hated surfing, and I hated having to ride the school bus from the beach to school each morning while all dirty from the beach. It didn't matter, though, that I had no interest. It was easiest for them, so I had no choice.

Schoolwork still didn't matter to me. It seemed like nothing in my world was allowed to matter to me, not even my family. I didn't see why I should care about what anyone else thought was important. I just wanted to go home . . . to my real home.

High school is harder to fake, though, and I started failing several classes right away. Some teachers would scold me for not doing my work. Some would just roll their eyes. Some seemed to not even notice. It wasn't until my Algebra 1 teacher, Mr. Parker, pulled me aside one day that I even started to consider the consequences of my choices. Mr. Parker didn't ask me about my homework or my grades. He asked what was going on in my life. No adult had ever asked me that before. I wasn't even sure how to answer the question.

I tried to give him some short answer just to blow him off, but he wouldn't let me. He said he could tell there was something going on and insisted that he wanted to understand. I told him about the surf team and how much I hated it. His suggestion was to quit the team, so I had to explain why I couldn't, that my foster family insisted on it or I wouldn't have a ride to school. I remember him looking me right in the eye and saying, "That sucks."

The next week he asked me to stay after class again, and he shared with me that he had had some tough times in high school. His situation wasn't the same as mine (his father had died and he had to drop out of baseball and go to work to help his mom pay the bills), and he never tried to compare his situation to mine. He just wanted me to know that there are ways to get through tough times.

About a month later, I missed three days of school in a row. We were back in court, with my parents fighting over custody again. This time, my biological father's parents were arguing that I should live with them in the next county. The third day in court I was sitting at the table and received a text message through the school's messaging system online. It was Mr. Parker wondering where I was and if I was okay.

He wasn't trying to hassle me about schoolwork or accuse me of ditching. He just wanted me to know that he was concerned. It was then that I really started to believe that he cared about me. Other teachers who had tried to force me into their expectations always seemed concerned about their work, or how I was making things hard for them. Mr. Parker, for some reason I can't quite explain, made me feel like he was concerned about me.

The court case ended with no change in my status. I was to continue living with the foster family that wanted me to act just like their own son did. My mom kept working two jobs even as my sisters who had graduated moved out of state to find work for themselves. She wanted me to come home, and so did I. The judge had other ideas.

When I returned to school, Mr. Parker pulled me aside and asked what had happened. He asked if he could message me more often, and if he could ask about my schoolwork in other classes. I told him he could, but I didn't know why I said that. I hated it when my foster family wanted to control me or insert themselves into my business. I think I doubted that Mr. Parker would even bother.

Boy was I wrong. Mr. Parker checked in with me each week. He was never happy when I hadn't done my work, especially major projects. But he never carried that over into a judgment about me. He focused on what I wanted and on what I needed to do to get there. He helped me decide that I wanted to join the army after graduation, and I don't think I would have graduated at all if he hadn't taken an interest. I started to think of him like a dad, and I was grateful he was always there, even when I screwed up. Mr. Parker didn't try to impose his structure on my life, the way my foster family had. He helped me see how I needed to build a structure for myself.

It wasn't easy, and I let him down a lot. Things with my foster family got worse, as their structure kept interfering with what I was trying to do for myself. I got a job at a restaurant down the street from our house bussing tables. I was proud that I was doing something for myself that put a little money in my pocket. They tried to make me quit, though, because I was expected to work weekends later than my curfew. I ignored them, and they threatened to send me back to Cherry Hill. They didn't follow through, but once they threatened that it made it clear to me that they didn't really care about me at all, as I had felt for a long time. They wanted me to be someone I wasn't.

Mr. Parker kept checking in on me, even the following year when I wasn't in his class. He helped me create a plan to make up credits for classes I had failed, and to see that I needed to plan for my future as well. Without his help, I wouldn't have made it to graduation.

Things with my mom got worse when my sisters moved out of state, and she developed some substance problems of her own. At some point, I realized that this meant there would be no chance of me returning home. The life I knew had been ripped away from me in one afternoon in a courtroom.

BRAIN RESEARCH AND LEARNING

This student grew up in a household where he experienced neglect, but he did not realize it until much later. His experience as a child was one of freedom and self-sufficiency; however, his freedom came at the cost of his schoolwork and academic achievement. This student was too young to understand how different his unstructured homelife was from his peers'.

Ideally, the foster-care system is designed to provide stability to youth whose backgrounds indicate a lack of structure. Sometimes, as seen in this case, the structure provided isn't welcome by the youth. Often, as in Matt's case, the provided structure focuses on the immediate physical needs of the child without taking into consideration his or her individual emotional needs or desires.

Other than at home, the other major component of a child's life where structure can be cultivated is at school. By its nature, the school environment is one where adults provide an organized schedule of activities designed to inculcate knowledge, social growth, and a sense of routine.

Social work researchers at California State University, San Jose, found that "the most important external factor" that moved foster youth toward postsecondary success "includes educational stability in high school coupled with a challenging high school curriculum" (Merdinger, Hines, Lemon Osterling, & Wyatt, 2005, p. 875). However, not every attempt to create structure and stability is effective with these youth, and often they are found in less-challenging curriculum because their grades have been poor, sometimes due to a lack of structure and support rather than a lack of ability.

In Matt's narrative, his seventh-grade teacher, Mrs. Knox, attempted to overcome his resistance to accept the expectations of school by getting angry and trying to "force" his compliance. The overall viability of this technique with any student is debatable; however, its success does depend on a student being familiar with a sense of disciplinary structure at home. Many children will try to avoid being yelled at because they have learned that changing their behavior can result in a removal of the negative stimulus (yelling). This is textbook operant conditioning (per Skinner, 1937).

However, such conditioning through negative reinforcement relies upon the child having learned that changing behavior will change the stimulus. In the case of children from homes with little structure, this behavior modification has often not been learned. Rather than changing behavior, the child sometimes finds that another way to eliminate the stimulus is simply to avoid or ignore the adult, which also results in a removal of the structuring influence the school day is designed to provide (see Skinner, 1936). For Matt, this returned him to a familiar state of independence, providing a positive reinforcement for continuing not to complete his schoolwork.

Mr. Parker's influence on Matt was different. Rather than approaching Matt as a figure of authority, Mr. Parker approached Matt in the role of a mentor. Many studies have shown that mentoring relationships have a positive influence on the current experience of youth in foster care as well as future success and well-being as adults (Ahrens et al., 2011; Blakeslee, 2015; Salazar, Roe, Ullrich, & Haggerty, 2016, among many others).

It is important to note that Mr. Parker's relationship with Matt was not a product of a typical structured mentoring application, where a youth is partnered with an adult specifically for the purpose of mentoring, such as with the Big Brothers and Big Sisters programs. Mr. Parker's behavior demonstrates a mentoring style known as Natural Mentoring.

A Natural Mentor is one that youth identify for themselves from within one of the social networks of their experience. The relationship is based on mutual trust and is built through a natural process similar to the development of a friendship, rather than artificially through the enrollment in a formal mentoring program.

However, just because the relationship is identified by the youth does not mean that the adult has no ability to cultivate such a relationship. The relationship between student and teacher is one that is fraught with an imbalanced power dynamic that, from the student's perspective, can eliminate the possibility of mentoring. This was true in the relationship between Matt and Mrs. Knox.

However, Mr. Parker made an effort to get to know Matt beyond the expectations of his classroom, which indicated to Matt that this was an adult who was interested in more than just his grades or lack of performance in class. For example, Mr. Parker' initial question of Matt wasn't about his homework or grades, but about Matt's life.

Mr. Parker had experienced difficulty in his own life, but rather than immediately relating those difficulties, which might imply that Matt's behavior wasn't up to par, Mr. Parker waited until a later date to relate a personal anecdote, showing Matt that he was interested in opening a line of communication and demonstrating an authentic interest in Matt's situation.

It is important to note that Mr. Parker only had a mentoring influence over Matt because Matt himself chose to allow that influence. However, Mr. Parker did not wait passively to be picked before extending the offer of help.

Students from homeless or foster backgrounds are sometimes reluctant to attempt a connection with an adult, out of fear of rejection, feelings of embarrassment, or not wanting to make their situation worse (Moore & McArthur, 2011). Mr. Parker's authentic interest in Matt's background and situation, whatever it may be, was a crucial signal to Matt that this was an adult who could provide guidance without personal judgment. Mr. Parker helped Matt discover how Matt himself could identify and reach his own goals.

Sometimes students whose experience has taught them that "the system" has failed them or tried to impose on them will close themselves off as a coping mechanism. These students can seem distant, reluctant to engage, and sometimes even antisocial. This means when making an approach to offer help, you may get shut down at first. Maintain the offer without seeking to impose it. You may have to approach the student several times before he or she begins to see that you are interested in knowing them and their situation.

Another technique successful Natural Mentors use is to ask questions rather than to provide advice. Teachers are used to telling students what to do, but, especially in the case of students like Matt, some students have been told what to do about so many things that they reject further attempts to interfere in their own thought processes, even if their thinking is flawed. Matt had lost control over a living situation that, while not ideal, was what he had grown used to.

The intake into the child welfare system took away all his possessions, his clothes, his own room, and, in the case of his first placement, even control over access to food and drink. This imposed lack of power over their own choices can result in foster youth acting out in ways that seem defiant (Hedin, Höjer, & Brunnberg, 2011).

Mr. Parker's approach of respecting Matt's prerogative to make choices, even ones that Mr. Parker might not agree with, established a new type of relationship with an adult than Matt had ever experienced before, one where Matt's self-determination was welcomed and nurtured. In this way, Mr. Parker was able to guide Matt to make choices that enabled him to success-fully transition to adulthood.

Matt's early experience of growing up was in a household that provided little structure for him, so as the child welfare system attempted to impose a structure on him, he rejected most of those attempts as efforts to control him.

By providing the opportunity for a relationship where Matt would be authentically respected for who he was, including his flaws, Mr. Parker allowed Matt to select a type of structure for his own life that he would not feel was imposed on him externally without regard to Matt's desires or emotional needs. Matt even described Mr. Parker's influence as "like a dad," indicating that it wasn't structure per se that Matt was rejecting, but rather the imposition of that structure by others rather than the building of it for himself.

CONCLUSION

Students who enter the foster-care system often feel as though the control they are used to feeling over their own lives has been stripped away by "the system." The last thing these students want is another system (i.e., the school or its representatives) attempting to force more compliance. This creates a challenge for the classroom teacher whose primary job relies upon the compliance of students.

The first thing to remember is that our students are people first. This might seem like a trite recommendation, but you will discover that in the midst of managing a teacher's workload, it can be easy to forget that our students' lives might be even more complicated than our own.

Finding a way to authentically connect with your students, especially those with some instability in their home lives, is key to finding a way to provide them the support they need. It can be tricky, but it will only work if the student chooses to allow you to provide that help. They must know it is available in order to accept it, so reaching out to them with interest in their personal lives can signal that you see them as more than a classroom complication.

The important thing is to provide a space where your student can feel comfortable sharing with you without violating the professional distance required to be maintained between teacher and student. This does not mean that you cannot be friendly and personal with your students, but protect your professional reputation by ensuring that you maintain some distance. Don Benjamín, an early twentieth-century maître'd from the Spanish television show *Gran Hotel*, would tell his waiters to keep *lo que mide un mostrador,* or the width of a counter, between themselves and guests. Teachers should keep the figurative distance of the teacher's desk.

READER TAKEAWAYS

- It is important to remember and respect that foster students experience a loss of control in their lives. Reactions to this loss can be to reject all attempts at structure or to embrace arenas where the student can continue to exercise personal control.
- Approaching the student with genuine concern about their struggles beyond your classroom can signal that you are an adult willing to help.
- Natural Mentoring is an effective way to guide these students to finding ways to provide structure in their own lives (see Bottomley, n.d.).
- Avoid comparing your experience with theirs, and never judge a student for his or her home situation.
- Try to avoid judging students for decisions they make, and help them see why making a different choice would benefit them more. Lead them to choose for themselves, rather than try to impose your own decisions upon them.
- Assumptions about what these students need are rarely helpful. Ask questions to help the student identify for themselves what they need.

REFERENCES

Ahrens, K. R., DuBois, D. L., Garrison, M., Spencer, R., Richardson, L. P., & Lozano, P. (2011). Qualitative exploration of relationships with important non-parental adults in the lives of youth in foster care. *Children and Youth Services Review, 33*(6), 1012–1023. doi:10.1016/j.childyouth.2011.01.006

Blakeslee, J. E. (2015). Measuring the support networks of transition-age foster youth: Preliminary validation of a social network assessment for research and practice. *Children and Youth Services Review, 52,* 123–134. doi:10.1016/j.childyouth.2015.03.014

Bottomley, L. (n.d.). What is a natural mentor? Retrieved June 2, 2019, from https://www.canr.msu.edu/news/what_is_a_natural_mentor

Hedin, L., Höjer, I., & Brunnberg, E. (2011). Settling into a new home as a teenager: About establishing social bonds in different types of foster families in Sweden. *Children and Youth Services Review, 33*(11), 2282–2289. doi:10.1016/j.childyouth.2011.07.016

Merdinger, J. M., Hines, A. M., Lemon, O. K., & Wyatt, P. (2005). Pathways to college for former foster youth: Understanding factors that contribute to educational success. *Child Welfare, 84*(6), 867–896.

Moore, T., & McArthur, M. (2011). "Good for kids": Children who have been homeless talk about school. *Australian Journal of Education, 55*(2), 147–160. doi:10.1177/000494411105500205

Salazar, A. M., Roe, S. S., Ullrich, J. S., & Haggerty, K. P. (2016). Professional and youth perspectives on higher education-focused interventions for youth transitioning from foster care. *Children and Youth Services Review, 64,* 23–34. doi:10.1016/j.childyouth.2016.02.027

Skinner, B. F. (1936). A failure to obtain "disinhibition." *The Journal of General Psychology, 14*(1), 127–135. doi:10.1080/00221309.1936.9713142

Skinner, B. F. (1937). Two types of conditioned reflex: A reply to Konorski and Miller. *The Journal of General Psychology, 16*(1), 272–279. doi:10.1080/00221309.1937.9917951

Chapter 2

"Is Mami Going to Leave Us?": Children Who Face Anxiety

Amber E. Wagnon, PhD

There is no separation of mind and emotions; emotions, thinking, and learning are all linked.

Eric Jensen

Expected Chapter Learning Outcomes:

- Readers will gain insight into the experiences of a college student who was faced with separation from her mother due to immigration.
- Readers will gain insight into how anxiety, stress, and separation fears impact students.

Educators are often faced with overwhelming tasks. In our current society, these tasks are not limited to the educational realm; instead, those in public education are expected to meet a child's social, emotional, and educational needs each day. We know that a student's home environment often dictates their actions, ability to learn, and their needs (Hemmeter, Ostrosky, & Fox, 2006).

However, details of the home environment and past events often remain unknown to many educators. Even when the circumstances are known, how to help a child is often beyond an educator's training. Though these feel like difficult odds, listening and working to understand human experiences can assist educators with meeting the needs of their students.

Consider the story that follows, recounted by a college freshman recalling the difficult time she and her family endured while waiting on her parents' immigration status. Would teachers have recognized any changes in her behavior? In what ways must educators acknowledge and approach the trauma that students whose parents are immigrants face as a result of possible separation from their guardians?

STUDENT NARRATIVE

Protection Papers

I sat quietly waiting for her to find the right prayer. Psalm 91. The protection prayer. That's really what we needed, protection. Protection from having our family ripped apart across a thousand miles. I didn't really understand that at the time. How could a six-year-old begin to grasp what being a "legal citizen" is?

"Mami, are we going to be okay? I don't want you to leave us," I asked lightly.

"Tienes que tener fe. No me voy a tener que ir, hija," my Mami consoled me. [You have to have faith. I am not going to have to leave.]

However, I knew we needed to pray and trust in our God that we'd be okay. I knew things had to turn out okay because I wanted my Mami to be able to stay. She was so full of hope and strength. Her dark brown eyes skimmed the words on the pages, concentrating with her signature scowl. She finally found the page and began reading.

> *If you say, "The Lord is my refuge,"*
> *and you make the Most High your dwelling,*
> *no harm will overtake you,*
> *no disaster will come near your tent.*
> *For he will command his angels concerning you*
> *to guard you in all your ways; [Psalm 91:9–11]*

Her reading was like a strong, melancholy tune and I could feel how much she meant every word. This became our ritual, our sacred moments. Oftentimes this was the highlight of my day because it brought my family closer despite the possibility of us being torn apart. We felt so much comfort when she read that protection prayer it was like we were in a shell and nothing could break into our moment. I would always follow along closely and try to understand what the words meant without having to stop and ask her. Though, she could always tell when something confused me, so she would explain briefly before moving on. When she finished the prayer, we would hug each other tight and say a quick goodnight. I always hoped this would not be our last goodnight, and I felt a bit better knowing we had said our protection prayer.

After a year of having heard this prayer, I learned to read it myself and understand what everything meant for us, for our family. My sister was now old enough to stay up until that time. She would stomp into the room with her chubby, little legs and struggle to get onto the raised bed. I began reading and let myself be taken by the meaning of my words. The prayer was not particularly long, but halfway through my sister would begin to doze off. I would have to hoist her off the bed and drag her along to get into our bed. We slept especially close together one night, and I felt my little sister shake my arm a bit. She had either woken up, or not yet fallen asleep, and asked, "Is Mami going to leave us?"

"No, Julie. That's why we read the prayer. She's going to stay," I promised. "Go back to sleep. Don't worry."

There was really no way of knowing how to move forward at that point. We had waited four years for her case to move forward, but there was always something else we needed to send. There was an interview that I remember was crucial but needed to be done in English. We worked on her speaking after the prayer. I taught what I could to the best of my ability. My mother laughed so carefree when something she said made no sense. I could only teach her simple things like, "My name is Maria," "I live in Porter, Texas," "I want to stay in America." We prayed a lot the day of the interview because that was the end of it. Either she was going to be able to stay, or she was going to have to go two hundred miles away and my father would raise us alone.

My aunt that had just been through the process with her mom a few years before told us that after the interview it is only a matter of waiting. The waiting started to feel like an eternity. What would happen if we got a letter saying she had to leave? Our daily prayer kept us hopeful and optimistic for the future. We had adopted a new daily routine: checking the mail. Every day, my mom would get out of the car and grab the mail. There was always so much anticipation for a letter that practically held my family's future. After over a year of nothing, my parents started losing hope, and checking the mail was dreadful. My mom would return to the car with a gloomy look on her face and no one dared to speak.

"The letter is in the mail today," I proudly proclaimed one day. There really was a letter. My mom had worked so hard for this, and in a split moment we were going to find out if it was worth it. My dad remained calm and collected, but my sister and I were flying out of our seats to know what was in the envelope. With shaking hands, my mother opened her letter and wept. Time stood still. Now what do we do? I could not believe this.

Through tears and sniffles, my mom began to read us the words that changed my family forever: "Welcome to the United States of America. . . . Your application for permanent residency has been approved."

BRAIN RESEARCH AND LEARNING

Valeria was lucky: her mother was granted American citizenship and she and her sister were protected by the fact that they were born following their family's immigration to the United States. Despite this positive outcome, research tells us that the possibility of separation impacted Valeria's brain, her education, and her life outlook. In fact, children who fear separation are often diagnosed with separation anxiety.

The central feature of "separation anxiety is excessive distress when faced with actual or perceived separation from people to whom the individual has a strong emotional attachment" (Redlich et al., 2015). Research asserts that "separation anxiety disorder is the most frequently diagnosed, accounting for up to 50% of referrals" (Battaglia et al., 2017, Bell-Dolan, 1995; Cartwright-Hatton, McNicol, & Doubleday, 2006).

This means that educators are likely to have a large number of students in their classrooms and schools who suffer from separation anxiety disorder and high levels of stress. While all children experience fears, like a fear of the dark, for children like Valeria the continuous threat of her mother's deportation persistently produced fear that "can have lifelong consequences by disrupting the developing architecture of the brain" (Shonkoff & Fox, 2011, p. 1).

Dr. Nathan A. Fox, PhD, and Dr. Jack Shonkoff, MD, assert that "chronic activation of the body's stress response systems has been shown to disrupt the efficiency of brain circuitry and lead to both immediate and long-term problems in learning, behavior, and both physical and mental health. This is especially true when stress system overload occurs during sensitive periods of early brain development" (2011, p. 1).

When a person is faced with anxiety, fear, or stress, different stress chemicals, including cortisol, begin to circulate within their body. Elevated cortisol levels impede a person's ability to concentrate, listen, and recall information (Shonkoff & Fox, 2014). Specific groups of students often struggle with anxiety.

For example, adolescents often "struggle to cope with the challenges of identity development" and this presents challenges as "learning to effectively respond to the emotional demands they encounter from day to day is essential to their success in school, work, and social settings" (Langelier & Connell, 2005, p. 1). These struggles can often lead to increased stress and anxiety.

Behavioral studies have also revealed that children of all ages with separation anxiety frequently have difficulty regulating their emotions and will seek out help in solving problems instead of attempting to solve these problems on their own (Redlich et al., 2015). Educators can implement activities like cooperative groups to enable students to develop more self-reliant skills (Duman, 2010).

Research further tells us that there is a useful method to work with students who are experiencing fears and anxiety: the "unlearning fear process," which must be utilized deliberately. According to Shonkoff and Fox (2014), "the unlearning process involves activity in the prefrontal cortex, which decreases the fear response by regulating the activity of the amygdala" and is an intervention that can be helpful for children facing fear and anxiety (p. 3).

With this intervention when a child is experiencing a fear or anxiety "providing additional explanations for anxious behavior during these controlled exposures has proven to be particularly successful" (p. 4). In other words, talking through the feelings of anxiety or fear often help a child learn to regulate such feelings.

CONCLUSION

While this chapter highlights the stress and anxiety faced by a child of an immigrant, the brain-based information from the chapter is easily transferable. Children are likely to experience stress, anxiety, and separation fears following a divorce, a death, a move, a placement in foster care, and many other situations. It is important that all educators recognize the scientific reasoning associated with the stress and anxiety these experiences can cause.

But what can educators do to assist their students when these issues arise? There are multiple strategies like facilitating writing opportunities, or teaching empathy through literature and art, but listening must come first. It is impossible for educators to effectively educate the whole student without first knowing their story. Scientific research shows that the brain can change, even after experiencing trauma and prolonged stress (Jensen, 2010). However, that change must be preceded by an educator who is willing to listen, understand the scientific research, and apply it to their student-educator interactions.

READER TAKEAWAYS

- Brain research confirms that students who face prolonged stress are more likely to struggle in the school setting.
- Educators have a duty and a responsibility to care for the whole student in order to teach the curriculum.
- When students experience anxiety and stress their bodies have scientific, biological reactions.

REFERENCES

Battaglia, M., Garon-Carrier, G., Côté, S. M., Dionne, G., Touchette, E., Vitaro, F., Boivin, M. (2017). Early childhood trajectories of separation anxiety: Bearing on mental health, academic achievement, and physical health from mid-childhood to preadolescence. *Depression and Anxiety, 34*(10), 918–927.

Bell-Dolan, D. (1995). Separation anxiety disorder. In R.T. Ammerman & M. Hersen (Eds.), *Handbook of child behavior therapy in the psychiatric setting.* New York, NY: Wiley.

Cartwright-Hatton, S., McNicol, K., & Doubleday, E. (2006). Anxiety in a neglected population: Prevalence of anxiety disorders in pre-adolescent children. *Clinical Psychology Review, 26*, 817–833.

Duman, B. (2010). The effects of brain-based learning on the academic achievement of students with different learning styles. *Educational Sciences: Theory and Practice, 10*(4), 2077–2103.

Hemmeter, M. L., Ostrosky, M., & Fox, L. (2006). Social and emotional foundations for early learning: A conceptual model for intervention. *School Psychology Review, 35*(4), 583–601.

Jensen, E. (2005). *Teaching with the brain in mind* (2nd ed., rev. and updated). Alexandria, VA: Association for Supervision and Curriculum Development.

Jensen, E. (2010). *Teaching with poverty in mind: What being poor does to kids brains and what schools can do about it.* Alexandria, VA: Association for Supervision and Curriculum Development.

Langelier, C. A., & Connell, J. D. (2005). Emotions and learning: Where brain based learning and cognitive-behavioral counseling strategies meet the road. *River College Online Academic Journal, 1*(1).

Redlich, R., Grotegerd, D., Opel, N., Kaufmann, C., Zwitserlood, P., Kugel, H., Dannlowski, U. (2015). Are you gonna leave me? Separation anxiety is associated with increased amygdala responsiveness and volume. *Social Cognitive and Affective Neuroscience, 10*(2), 278–284.

Shonkoff, J. P., & Fox, N. (2012). *National Scientific Council on the Developing Child (2005/2014). Excessive stress disrupts the architecture of the developing brain*(Working Paper No. 3; updated edition). Retrieved from www.developing child.harvard.edu

Shonkoff, J. P., & Fox, N. (2014). *National Scientific Council on the Developing Child (22014). Excessive stress disrupts the architecture of the developing brain* (Working Paper No. 3; updated edition). Retrieved from www.developingchild.harvard.edu

Shonkoff, J. P., & Garner, A. S. (2012). The lifelong effects of early childhood adversity and toxic stress. *Pediatrics, 129*(1), e232.

Chapter 3

The Struggle of Attention-Deficit/ Hyperactivity Disorder

Jennifer Rumsey, PhD

Why fit in when you were born to stand out?

Dr. Seuss

Expected Chapter Learning Outcomes:

- Readers will gain insight into what life is like for a middle school girl struggling with attention-deficit/hyperactivity disorder.
- Readers will be provided with brain research about attention-deficit/hyperactivity disorder (ADHD).

STUDENT NARRATIVE

My favorite attention-deficit/hyperactivity disorder (ADHD) quote is "I have more thoughts before breakfast than most people do all day." My brain is always working, always thinking, coming up with great ideas for my next drawing, singing one of my favorite songs, creating ideas for the next fan fic I am going to write. That's why my mom calls me The Princess of Creativity—I am always being creative, and it is the best thing about me. I am the only 14-year-old that I know who still has a really great imagination.

It's like my ADHD brain gave me a creativity super power. I am really good at drawing, writing stories, singing, and making up new ways to do things. But my ADHD brain is not easy to deal with because all of the creative thoughts never stop, and I have a hard time staying focused on anything except what my creative brain wants to think about.

I like school, mostly, but it is hard for me. I really started having trouble in fourth grade. One of the things I remember most is my math teacher getting frustrated with me because I wasn't paying attention. I would try to pay attention in school, but it was very difficult, and it still is. One part of my brain was trying to focus on math, but then the other part was thinking about drawing, and I would end up drawing horse pictures because all of my friends loved them, and I was obsessed with riding horses and watching My Little Pony.

Math has always been harder for me than reading and writing, and math got really hard in fourth grade. I had a hard time remembering my addition and subtraction math facts, and then we had to learn multiplication. My mom bought me flash cards, and we practiced multiplication. I would get them all correct, but then it's like the numbers would seep out of my memory, and when I would try to do multiplication in class, I had forgotten most of them, especially the hard ones like 6's, 7's, and 8's. I'm in eighth grade now, and to be honest, I still can't remember all of my multiplication facts sometimes.

Fourth grade was when my doctor diagnosed me with ADHD, and I wasn't surprised. My older brother Jack has ADHD, but he has the super hyperactive kind, and he had to take a pill. My parents didn't want me to take a pill for my ADHD because it had some bad effects on my brother. The pill made him not want to eat, and he had trouble sleeping too, but they knew that if Jack didn't take his pill, he would be in trouble at school every day. So my parents decided that I wouldn't take the pill, but they went to my school and set me up with a 504 plan.

Fifth grade was one of the worst times I had at school. The whole year was really hard. I had a lot of friends, but I did not do very well in my classes. Even though I had a 504 plan, it just seemed like my teachers did not care about it, or they did not know how to work with a kid like me.

One time that year, I was in social studies, and I must have gotten distracted because I started drawing. My teacher, Mrs. Shapiro, snatched the drawing off of my desk, wadded it up, and threw it away. Then she yelled at me in front of everyone in the class and made me go sit in the hall. I was so embarrassed and sad. I was mad at myself for not paying attention, and it made me cry to remember her mean voice and face. She left me out in the hall for at least twenty minutes.

I have kind of gotten used to my teachers getting annoyed or frustrated or mad at me. I forget to finish my class work sometimes, and sometimes I forget to turn in my homework. My ADHD brain makes me scattered, forgetful, and disorganized. A perfect example of this happened this year, eighth grade. I have one big binder for all of my classes, and I brought it to my science class. Then, I saw that everyone had laptops out, and I started to panic because I thought I had left my laptop in my locker.

I asked my teacher if I could run to my locker to get it, and Mr. Tinney was not happy about it. He gave me a look and said, "You need to come prepared to class" in an irritated way. I rushed out to get the laptop, but when I opened my locker, it wasn't in there. I started to feel my heart racing and my breathing got faster. I was panicking. Where had I left my laptop? I searched my backpack that was hanging in my locker, but no laptop was inside. I started worrying that I had left my laptop in another class, but I could not remember where.

I forced myself not to cry as I went back inside of my science class without my laptop. Luckily, Mr. Tinney did not really focus on me coming in, so I just sort of slunk back to my desk and sat down. Other kids in my class were staring at me, and my friend asked me what was wrong. I just shook my head and let my long hair cover my face as I opened my binder. Stupid ADHD brain! My laptop was inside of my binder; I had it with me all along.

The worst is when I haven't been paying attention and a teacher calls on me, and I have no clue if what I answer is right. When it's obvious that I don't know what the teacher is talking about, or if I have to ask directions on what we are supposed to be doing, sometimes the teacher gets mad at me. Sometimes the kids in my class laugh at me, and I just want to run away or hide or something. I get so angry with myself too. I tell myself that I am stupid and other mean things. I started having a lot of anxiety last year. I worry about losing my friends, or I get stressed out about having to take a test, or I get upset thinking about people in class looking at me and judging me. I have had to leave class and run to the restroom a few times because I was having a panic attack. My parents know about it, and I have been going to see a counselor for my anxiety.

My ADHD makes it hard for me to feel normal, and I constantly think that other people think that I am stupid or weird. I get so frustrated with myself, and I have tried to accept that no matter what I do, I will always be really different because of my ADHD brain. I try to ask to sit in the back of the room so people in my classes aren't looking at me as much, but most of my teachers make me sit near the front. Feeling different and stupid is really hard on me.

One thing that people don't understand about ADHD is how much it tires me out. It's hard to try to focus and pay attention all day at school and worry about people thinking I'm dumb or worry that I will forget something. It's like I'm fighting with myself just so I can do good at school. By the end of each day, I am so ready to get home and relax and stop fighting to focus. The worst part of my day is always when I have to do homework. I had to do school all day, and it is always hard, and now I have to do school at home too?

My parents have tried lots of different ways to motivate me to do my homework, but I still get so frustrated that I have homework at all. I just want to be at home, finally relaxing from the stress of trying to do okay in school. I want to draw and sing and create.

When I was younger, homework would make me really angry, and sometimes I would argue with my parents about having to do it. I would try anything to get out of doing homework, and I even lied about it on and off. I am better about homework now, but it still makes me unhappy that I have to do more school when I am at home. I need a break to be myself and do what makes me happy.

Another thing that most people don't understand about ADHD is that I don't just struggle with school—there are other things that my ADHD brain is not very good at. Like keeping up with things, or picking up messes. I am very disorganized. My mom still has to help me clean my room, and she tries to teach me the way to put my stuff where I can find it. I lose everything! I can literally just be using my hairbrush, and a minute later I have no idea where I put it. Losing things makes me extremely frustrated and very angry with myself.

For example, this spring break I was going to stay with my grandparents in Florida for the week, and I told my mom that I did not need any help packing. I felt proud of myself because I made a list of all of the things I might need for a fun beach trip, and I thought I had packed everything. I made sure to get my phone charger too because that is one thing I forget or lose a lot.

My dad was sitting with me in the airport at the gate for my flight, when I realized that I did not know where my phone was. I started to have serious anxiety about my phone. Did I leave it somewhere in the airport? I frantically dug through my purse and my suitcase. My dad was telling me to calm down, that it would all be fine, but my phone was nowhere to be found. Thinking about it, I knew that I had not used my phone in the car on the way to the airport. My dad called my brother, and told him to see if he heard my phone when my dad called it. Sure enough—I had left my phone in my bedroom!

I had to spend all of spring break without my phone, and I was angry with myself for the whole week. I still had fun, but I spent a lot of the time in Florida yelling at myself for being so forgetful.

Next year, I start high school, and I told my parents that I think I should try taking medication for my ADHD. I did my own research, and I think a non-stimulant will be the best type of medicine for me. I do not want to make bad grades in high school. I know that I want to go to college, and I have to do well in high school to get accepted to a decent college or university. Plus, I am so tired of fighting with myself to focus in class.

My creativity is still really strong. My drawing abilities keep improving, and I have developed my own art style; I get a lot of compliments on it. In the past two years, I taught myself how to play the guitar and the ukulele. My dad tells me all of the time that I am a natural with music, and I guess he is right. Learning the guitar and ukulele were really easy for me. My singing has gotten very strong. I am performing with my voice coach and her band this upcoming weekend. And, I am super excited that I have the lead in the school musical this month.

Right now, my latest obsession is everything Broadway. Musicals give me lots of joy. I plan on getting a degree in musical theater in college, and my mom has talked to me about which colleges have the best musical theater departments. I know that I am lucky in some ways to have my creative ADHD brain, but there are so many things about it that have made my life really hard. I wish more people, especially teachers, understood what a struggle living with ADHD really is.

BRAIN RESEARCH AND LEARNING

ADHD is the most commonly diagnosed neurodevelopmental disorder of school-aged children in the United States. The Centers for Disease Control and Prevention (2018) estimates that 11 percent of children aged 4–17 years are diagnosed with this disorder.

There are three types of ADHDs, and the diagnosis of these disorders depends on which symptoms are the most prevalent. The most commonly identified type of ADHD is the inattentive type. When a child is diagnosed with the inattentive type of ADHD, she struggles to remain focused, has difficulty with organization or keeping up with things, struggles to begin or complete tasks, and is often inattentive (Centers for Disease Control and Prevention, 2018).

The second type of ADHD is the hyperactive type. Boys are much more likely to be diagnosed with and exhibit symptoms of the hyperactive type of ADHD than girls. If a child is diagnosed with the hyperactive form of ADHD, he exhibits high energy levels, struggles to sit still, blurts out or makes noises, runs around at inappropriate times, and acts impulsively (Centers for Disease Control and Prevention, 2018). A combination of inattention and hyperactivity constitutes the third type of ADHD.

The student presented in the narrative portion of this chapter was diagnosed with the inattentive type of ADHD. The academic challenges that she shared are typical of a teen with ADHD. The American Academy of Pediatrics explains that ADHD "can profoundly affect the academic achievement, well-being, and social interactions of children" (2011). In fact, youth with ADHD are often identified as having a coexisting, limiting condition.

The American Academy of Pediatrics (2011) recommends that primary care physicians, when evaluating a child with ADHD, also assess the child for learning disabilities, emotional or behavioral disorders (e.g., depression, anxiety, and oppositional defiant disorder), and other neurological disorders including Tourette's Syndrome.

The Centers for Disease Control and Prevention (2018) reports that almost half of the youth identified as having ADHD will also suffer from a learning disability: dyslexia (trouble reading), dysgraphia (trouble writing), or dyscalculia (trouble with math).

The young lady in this chapter suffers from anxiety that onset when she began going through puberty. One in five youth with ADHD will also struggle with anxiety and/or depression (Centers for Disease Control and Prevention, 2018).

Although more research on the causes of ADHD is needed, this neurological disorder is genetic. If a child is diagnosed with ADHD, it is highly likely that one of his parents also has ADHD (Centers for Disease Control and Prevention, 2018). Children and teens with ADHD have brain-functioning impairments that impact a brain's executive functioning skills. Executive functioning skills are those skills and abilities relating to time management, organization, focus, and attention.

Dr. Sharon Saline, a psychotherapist with extensive experience working with children who have ADHD, explains that children with ADHD have areas of the brain that are developmentally delayed as compared to their peers. This delay impacts how a child with ADHD acquires executive functioning skills. With impaired executive functioning, ADHD children are forgetful, inattentive, and disorganized (2018).

The Centers for Disease Control and Prevention (2018) and the American Academy of Pediatrics (2011) recommend a treatment plan for children who are diagnosed with ADHD that includes FDA-approved stimulant or non-stimulant medication, as well as behavior therapy that should occur both at home and at school.

Unfortunately, although stimulant medications are effective in helping curb hyperactivity and impulsivity as well as promoting the ability for an ADHD child to focus, these medications come with negative side effects. Side effects include sleeplessness, lack of appetite, moodiness, and, in some cases, hallucinations. Parents of a child with ADHD face the difficult decision of putting their child on medication. The side effects can be very challenging to deal with, and some children and teens hate the way medication affects them.

Training on how to implement behavior therapy is beneficial to parents when assisting their children at home. Although the Centers for Disease Control and Prevention and American Academy of Pediatrics recommend behavior therapy at school, all too often, teachers are not properly educated about ADHD or trained in best practices for working with ADHD children and teens.

In fact, Poznanski, Hart, and Cramer (2018) found that there are significant deficits in preservice teachers' knowledge about the symptoms of and treatment for ADHD. The researchers also found that preservice teachers lacked knowledge of effective classroom management techniques for working with ADHD students.

Although ADHD is the most commonly diagnosed neurological disorder in school-aged children, many teachers have had no formal training on this pervasive condition, nor do most teachers participate in any professional development addressing ADHD. Bell, Long, Garvan, and Bussing (2011) found that 77 percent of practicing teachers had no opportunity to learn about ADHD in their formal teacher training.

Even with the medication as a part of the treatment for this disorder, ADHD causes children to behave in ways that do not fit in the current expectations for students in public schools, and they are often punished as a result.

Impulsivity may cause children to blurt out in class, interrupt peers and the teacher, and say inappropriate or rude things. Inattentiveness can hinder a child's or adolescent's ability to follow teacher instructions and focus on the material being taught. Children with ADHD struggle with memory and organization, frequently losing necessary materials or forgetting assignment due dates and guidelines.

Finally, overactivity can cause students with ADHD to wander around rather than remain seated, to tap their feet, hands, or pencil, to hum, and to play with objects. Kos, Richdale, and Hay (2006) found that all of these types of ADHD behaviors are considered disruptive and/or disrespectful in a classroom environment. All too often, children and teens with ADHD see school as a dreaded place, filled with constant negative feedback and criticism.

Sadly, there is a stigma associated with ADHD. Kos et al. (2006) discussed how children and adolescents with ADHD are faced with negative responses from their peers, their teachers, and sometimes even their parents.

Teachers can have negative perceptions of students with ADHD, fearing that students with ADHD will be disruptive in the classroom and hard to teach. Bell et al. (2011) found that some teachers were unwilling to implement best practices to reach these students and unwilling to modify assignments to work with ADHD students' needs. The adverse views that teachers have of students with ADHD can negatively influence a child's peers as well as create a deleterious expectation that the disabled student ends up fulfilling.

In conclusion, children and adolescents with ADHD experience social, academic, and emotional problems as a result of this disorder. Despite its pervasiveness, most teachers have little to no training on the facts about ADHD or on the best methods and accommodations to implement for student success.

CONCLUSION

The young lady in the student narrative presents the difficulties that a teenager with the inattentive type of ADHD faces. However, her story is not reflective of all of the students struggling with ADHD that teachers will encounter in their classrooms. The girl in this narrative comes from a supportive, middle-class home with parents who are educated about her condition and who have the means to advocate for her right to an equitable education.

Tragically, many of the young people navigating the challenges of ADHD today do not have the same supports or privileges as the girl in the student narrative, as they may come from families fighting just to survive in poverty. Even with a 504 plan and parents who are her biggest advocate, the teen in the student narrative encountered teachers who treated her with less than a compassionate, supportive manner.

It is clear that some teachers view students who struggle with ADHD as a hassle, and many teachers lack basic knowledge about this very pervasive disorder. The reality is that ADHD is the most commonly diagnosed neurological disorder in children and teenagers, and the stigma of ADHD will only be defeated when teachers are widely educated about its causes as well as taught to implement best practices to create an equitable learning environment for their students with ADHD.

READER TAKEAWAYS

- ADHD is the most commonly diagnosed neurological disorder in school-aged children.
- Children and teens with ADHD are likely to be diagnosed with an additional learning disability and/or another emotional disorder or behavioral disorder.
- ADHD can negatively impact a child's academic achievement, social success, and emotional well-being.
- In order to effectively teach and help students with ADHD, teachers need to be educated about ADHD and trained in best practices to support the success of all of their students.

REFERENCES

American Academy of Pediatrics. (2011). ADHD: Clinical practice guidelines for the diagnosis, evaluation, and treatment of attention-deficit/hyperactivity disorder in children and adolescents. *Pediatrics, 128*(5). doi:10.1542/peds.2011-2654

Bell, L., Long, S., Garvan, C., & Bussing, R. (2011). The impact of teacher credentials on ADHD stigma perceptions. *Psychology in the Schools, 48*(2), 184–197. doi:10.1002/pits.20536

Centers for Disease Control and Prevention. (2018). *Attention deficit/hyperactivity disorder (ADHD)*. Retrieved from https://www.cdc.gov/ncbddd/adhd/index.html

Kos, J., Richdale, A., & Hay, D. (2006). Children with attention deficit hyperactivity disorder and their teachers: A review of the literature. *International Journal of Disability, Development & Education, 53*(2), 147–160. doi:10.1080/10349120600716125

Poznanski, B., Hart, K., & Cramer, E. (2018). Are teachers ready? Preservice teacher knowledge of classroom management and ADHD. *School Mental Health, 10*, 301–313. doi:10.1007/s12310-018-9259-2

Saline, S. (2018). *What your ADHD child wishes you knew*. New York, NY: TarcherPerigee.

Zentall, S., & Javorsky, J. (2007). Professional development for teachers of students with ADHD and characteristics of ADHD. *Behavioral Disorders, 32*(2), 78–93.

Chapter 4

From Trauma to Trafficking

Derek R. Riddle, PhD

Look in my eyes.
Tell me what they say.
Do they tell you my future?
Or just about today?
Can you see the tears I cry?
Well what about the pain I hide?
Or is it you just don't care what's inside.
All anyone ever sees
is the fake me I have to be.
But if that's all you want to see
then you'll never know
the real me.

Monique

Expected Chapter Learning Outcomes:

- Readers will be able to analyze the social, emotional, and cognitive factors connected to a woman's experiences that led to her becoming a victim of human trafficking.
- Readers will identify strategies that may support and mitigate students from becoming victims of human trafficking.

In 2017, the National Human Trafficking Hotline (NHTH), a national anti-trafficking hotline serving victims and survivors of human-trafficking and the anti-trafficking community in the United States, received a total of 26,557 phone calls and of those phone calls 8,524 were reported as human-trafficking cases. The NHTH has been collecting and reporting human-trafficking data since 2007 and since that time have reported an estimated

45,000 cases of human trafficking in the United States. Additionally, the Bureau of Justice Statistics (2011) reported that 95 percent of human-trafficking victims were women and over half were 17 years old or younger. Finally, the 2017 Federal Human Trafficking Report found that 95 percent of their cases involved sex trafficking (The Human Trafficking Institute, 2017). Unfortunately, these "data do not define the totality of human trafficking or of a trafficking network in any given area" (NHTH, n.d., "Hotline statistics," para. 1). It goes without saying that human trafficking has become a major problem facing adolescent women in the United States.

The Trafficking Victims Protection Act of 2000 defines sex trafficking as "a commercial sex act is induced by force, fraud, or coercion, or in which the person induced to perform such an act has not attained 18 years of age" (p. 5). While there are divergent ways to lure in individuals to sex trafficking, often, to those unaware of sex trafficking, this phenomenon and the causes leading up to it may seem puzzling. How does this heinous crime happen? Why do those victims just not run away? What more could have been done to prevent this from happening?

These questions and the answers to such questions have implications for those who work closely with young women, especially educators. In order to begin to shed light and provide insight to some of these questions, the following story provides the perspective of a victim of human trafficking. For confidentiality purposes, she has been given the pseudonym of Chloe. As this story unfolds, reflect and consider how Chloe's story can begin to provide the much-needed insight to potentially mitigate and/or prevent further acts of sex trafficking from occurring. Also, consider how her story can affect the work of educators and others whom work with young women at-risk of becoming a victim of sex trafficking.

CHLOE'S NARRATIVE

The following narrative will be organized in the following manner. First, Chloe's narrative will be divided into four sections: Being Groomed, Being Trafficked, Getting Out, and Going Back In. After her narrative, there will then be a brief discussion elaborating on the social emotional and cognitive learning and development applicable to this case. The intent is to understand these concepts connected to Chloe's case in order to be able to apply these concepts in other cases similar to Chloe's case.

Being Groomed

I was raised right here in [a place in the United States]. My mother and my father they were never married. They were in just a more of a boyfriend–girlfriend relationship. My father had been previously married as had been my mother. They were in their late twenties, so I think that both of them were in a place where, just coming out of recently being divorced, both of them really just wanted to have companionship with no commitment. Unfortunately, my father did not know all the details of my mother's past.

My mother [. . .] had experienced an extreme amount of trauma growing up. She had been severely abused as a child and adolescence, sexually, physically, and emotionally. That brought her a lot of unhealthy coping behaviors of her own. Prior to meeting my father, my mother had already been involved in sex trafficking. She was not currently using narcotics when she met my father but did have a previous issue with addiction. These are things, like I said, he was unaware of. They dated for probably almost two years.

They ended up moving in together [. . . .] Shortly after moving in, my mother found out she was pregnant with me [. . . .] and so enters me into the situation.

Now, although my mother has been sober prior to getting pregnant [. . . .] I was born addicted to opioids. My mother, part of her trauma, happened in her childhood all the way through her late teens. There was some extensive trauma that happened at the hands of a husband with whom she also had two other children. For whatever reason, again we don't ever know how trauma is going to manifest itself, what I do believe happened, for whatever reason, getting pregnant triggered her. My mother let herself back into her own spiral of unhealthy coping behaviors, which led to an opioid addiction.

Right there and then that is when the cat got out of the bag. I was born addicted, so then my father found out. My dad and my mother tried to work through it for about the next three or four months or so, but it was kind of too late. My mother, once she got a taste of that, was back out into that lifestyle again. I was probably about three or four months old. My understanding is that my mother left—was supposed to go to the store. She left to go get some milk, bread, whatever and did not come back.

About four days later, she shows back up. Her and my father have some sort of verbal altercation, and my father reiterates to her with the force of law enforcement and other people that she would not get me. That was not going to happen. So, my mother disappeared from my life until I'm about five years old.

About 5 years old though, she comes back. My father starts letting me see her [. . . .] One of the memories I talked about was—I had to be about 5 years old, and I wake up and my mother had made a pallet beside her bed and she was in bed with a strange man. I remember laying there, being very still, almost just pretending to still be asleep [. . . .] and just waiting for whatever they are doing to be done.

My dad finds out (probably me, right—five years old) and I don't see my mom again. I don't see my mom again until I'm about 10. When I am about

10, she again gets out of prison on one of the many instances that she gets in prison [. . . .] My dad lets me see her again. What has changed, at this point in my life, is that I'm a little bit smarter [. . . .] I realized that if I tell my father what I see then I don't get to see my mother.

Between 10 and 13, I'm observing my mother literally turning trick, doing drugs, you know, all these things. I will honestly say that nothing physically ever happened to me during that time. Nobody touched me or abused me or anything like that, but I was seeing this [. . . .] I was watching my mother finesse men, get money, and just—you know, but at the same time nothing is truly happening to me. As far as my dad is concerned, everything is great! Mom's great; mom's sober. Things are great, you know! And I would get to see her.

By 13, though [. . .] I am becoming very angry. Very angry! I'm acting out! [. . . .] I am just acting out in a thousand different ways: talking back and all those good things. I'm beginning to I think—mentally, begin to experiment with other lifestyle choices. You know just thinking about . . . you know, just getting really ugly. By the time I was 13, I ran away for the first time.

Couple weeks after my 16th birthday, I am pregnant [. . . .] My father does totally the opposite of what I think he should do [. . . .] He was very support-ive [. . .] He took me in and took care of me and my son [. . . .] Everything was good until my son was probably about ten months to a year old.

So now, I am 17 years old, getting ready to push 18. That anger—all that old stuff starts creeping back in. On top of it, I also think I wanted to be a teenager. I'm super naive. You put all the different factors of that in together. The old me started to emerge.

One of the defining moments I remember: it's probably got to be 10–11 o'clock at night. I put my son in the car seat, and I was getting ready to go out the front door. And my father got in between me and the door and he sim-ply shut the door (and I'm sure he asked me before: Where you going? What are you doing?) and I was going to go with friends and take off. And he just looked at me, and he grabbed the car seat out of my hand that had my infant son in it, and he stepped away from the door and opened it [. . . .] My son stayed and I left [. . . .] I would walk out that door with literally nowhere to go [. . . .] I went to my mom.

One thing that is important to understand about my story and my mother is that my mother was always very articulate. In her youth, she was very beautiful—a lot of fun to be around. My mom was that girl you know that everybody wanted to be her friend. When she talked to you, you listened. She was just very charismatic and totally awesome as far as that goes [. . . .] I definitely have that same type of personality. I'm an extrovert. I've always been the life of the party, very talkative and that really emerged during that time [. . . .] Everything I've seen my mother do—and mind you, just like any kid—I had built this fantasy that she was my hero.

I didn't see her drug habits [. . . .] I didn't see all those things. All that was somebody else's fault, right? It was the connection's fault. It was my stepfather (so I didn't know at the time but I now know it was her trafficker who she had married when I was 4 years old). It was all their fault. Everybody else: the system, the police department, the prison. When she went to jail, it was somebody else's is fault.

I built all these excuses and reasonings in my head. So, when I began to watch her, everything she did was about her body and her personality and that was how she got money [. . . .] I would just stand to really model that.

Within a few short months, being at my mom's [. . .] she would bring guys over that were there to hang out with her and I don't know when it exactly happened but I quickly realized that it would take me sitting at the kitchen table for fifteen minutes with me in a little half top and little shorts. They're handing me $100, buying me McDonalds, and asking me if there is anywhere that I need to go, if that makes sense. So, it is kind of like that sugar daddy thing has emerged.

I am not having sex with anybody. I am not prostituting myself. I am nothing like my mother, who is at this point a full-on prostitute. I'm not like her at all [. . . .] but I'm a gold digger. That's it! If I'm going to smile and wink at you, it is going to cost you some money.

Within three or four months, I am stripping. That is where everything changed.

Being Trafficked

A man who came over. It was a connection, and he was, again, typical trafficker that we know now. Flashy car, flashy clothes. He was young. He was only in his late twenties. So now he is more my age. He was there initially to deliver drugs to my mom, but he just totally blew me away.

At one point, he actually took me to a hip-hop concert where I didn't just get to go backstage, I got to go back to the hotel and hang out with the R&B stars that were here in [a place in the United States] doing a concert. I mean this guy was so connected he just blew my mind.

So a few weeks later, he tells me that he had basically what I consider a deal of a lifetime. I was going to go down to [a place in the United States] with him, I was going to entertain some men, and basically come back with all this money. And as crazy as this sounds, that is about as deep as I thought about it [. . . .] Unfortunately, only within a few hours of arriving there, we check into a hotel [. . . .] Everything changed kind of like immediately. What I remember is just walking into that hotel room, him tossing condoms on a bed, and him beginning to tell me basically what the next few hours or day was going to look like [. . . .] I believe, at that point, I probably began to backpedal a little and say oh, you know, NO on whatever level.

That is when I got hit. That first blow. Quite frankly the next—I don't know—few days, weeks, I went through what I now know is the breaking process.[1] *I was tortured and with every word of what that means: I mean . . . sexually . . . I was broken [. . . .] That is what the next ten months of my life was like.*

Getting Out

Ten months later, I would be in a place where I just wanted to die. Instead of killing myself, which I didn't have the courage to do [. . . .] At this point, I make a run for it [. . . .] I had made a couple attempts prior to this, just so you know to leave [. . . .] I jumped on a Greyhound bus; I came back here to [a city in the United States][. . .]

There was an officer over that 10 months who had been involved in my situation [. . . .] who would have interactions with me and when he would, not sexual, but when he would see me out there and stop me. I don't know how to explain it other than all I can say it was the first time during that period of time when somebody looked at me like I was a human [. . . .] He would always tell me, "You do not need to be here. Is there somebody I can call?" And I would never tell him nothing [sic]; I was totally terrified of him. I remember there was an officer down in [a city in the United States] that actually tricked me and this is in the beginning, in the breaking process, where he works at the traffickers a lot of officers did down there. I had been asked if I wanted help, if I wanted to get out, and that was a trick question and then told back to the trafficker. I did not trust that at all.

Anyway, this officer was a beat cop out there. He was a rookie cop, and I would see him all the time. Any time I seen him I was trying to go to jail [. . . .] This is going to sound crazy, but in the midst of everything that I'm telling you was that [that] jail was a reprieve for me.

I knew the only thing I could do was find that officer. So, I knew if I found that officer, I would have some reprieve or at least in my mind. I was finally going to do this and I didn't know where police headquarters was. I had never been to the police department itself. I have been to jail and the courthouse right, so I only knew where the jail in the courthouse were where they took me. So that's where I ran. I ended up making it into the courthouse, found my way downstairs, ran up to a counter and told a lady who I was looking for and of course she asked me my name and birthdate and when she did, she disclosed that I had about twelve warrants for my arrest.

I was arrested and this time I was booked under my middle name and my last name [. . . .] He [the trafficker] didn't know I was there. He couldn't find me [. . . .] Back then you actually had to call the jail, give the person's name, and the best thing about this [. . . .] I knew with confidence when I got booked under that alias, which was there accident. So instead of [Chloe's real name] they booked me under [a different name]. That no matter what, if he called—even with my birthday—because if he calls on the phone looking for a [Chloe's real name], they are going to say, "Well, give me her birthday." Because those are the two requirements and if he's going to give the birthday, they're going to say no [. . . .] It was awesome!

Within a few days—within a few weeks [. . . .] I found the courage to call my dad. For the first time in ten months, I called and my dad came down to the jail [. . . .] I just told him. I told him everything! Everything that that had happened.

My dad is awesome [. . . .] He just told me basically that I didn't have to worry about anything. He was going to take care of it. He didn't blame me. He didn't say I told you [. . . .] He took what happened to me very seriously [. . . .] My father came and got me and [. . .] relocated me to [a city in the United States].

Going Back In

Unfortunately, within a short period of time, I started experiencing that same girl that I told you about before that was articulate and smart and funny and fun to be around, totally disappeared. I became everything I told you about in the beginning [. . . .] I was totally socially awkward. I couldn't function in public. I would have a tough time breathing; all the physical ailments started coming up. Thinking that I have heart problems. What I now know is that I was experiencing extreme, complex Post Traumatic Stress Disorder (PTSD) and I was having triggers all over the place [. . . .] I was basically terrified out of my mind 24/7.

Within two years, I succumb to an addiction. I had a neighbor that introduced me to methamphetamine. That literally, in a matter of minutes, changed my life. The methamphetamine alleviated me and anesthetized me, and I went from everything I just told you to completely numb. And I would hold on to that for about 5 years.

I came back to my father's for a short period of time, but again I have a meth addiction now so within a very short period of time, maybe a few weeks, my dad took my son again [. . . .] He took my son, and me and my daughter went to my mother's. But now, the game changed. She was no longer my hero.

I was very angry. I was very dark [. . . .] Now, she is the enemy. Now, I almost victimize her if that makes sense. I just really didn't like her. I would talk about her, you know. I begin to sell drugs and eventually begin to sell back into, not only trafficking myself but others.

That only lasted a very short period of time and in 2008, I was looking at a very lengthy prison sentence. So, in December 2008, I went to jail. I was in a holding cell [. . . .] The first time in this whole story, I fell on my face and I cried out and I cried out to God and I went to the only thing since I knew since I was a little girl and I just began to pray that God would intervene [sic].

At this point in my life, nobody wanted to talk to me. I didn't have my father. I didn't have my mother. I didn't have anybody. I was losing my children, and in that five years, I would give birth to two more kids. So, I had a total of four children now. I only had three because my son would not come back at that point.

So, I have three daughters and I'm a hot mess [. . . .] I was that cliché girl [. . . .] That 25-year-old girl with tattoos, upset, methed out, kids are in CPS, but nobody knows the backstory. Well, plenty of people know the backstory, but nobody that is seeing me knows the backstory.

I did not go to prison; the judge had mercy on me. I only ended up serving ninety days. He gave me a second chance [. . . .] I cried out to my father that I would change my ways. He did not necessarily believe me, but he did love me and love my children, so he did allow me to come back out to a property that he had out here in the country in [a city in the United States] and live in a house that he had here. That is where everything changed.

I started—I got a job; I started going to school. I started attending church. I started working my way out of that.

BRAIN RESEARCH AND LEARNING

In order to understand Chloe's case and other cases potentially similar to hers, certain mitigating factors need to be discussed in order to understand the causality of her actions. Knowing these factors and their effects may assist those working with young people, like Chloe, to intervene in effective ways.

First and foremost, being abandoned by her mother at a young age, being woken at 5 years old to her mother "in bed with a strange man," and consequently having her mother removed from her life again caused Chloe to experience what is termed as complex childhood trauma. This type of trauma is when a child has witnessed "a frightening, dangerous, or violent event that poses a threat" (The National Child Traumatic Stress Network, n.d., "About Child Trauma," para. 1) and where she had "been exposed to one or more traumas over the course of [her life]" (The National Child Traumatic Stress Network, n.d., "What is Childhood Stress?," para. 1). As a result of experiencing complex childhood trauma, Chloe suffered the effects resulting from it.

There are varying effects of complex childhood trauma. The effects range from social and emotional responses to physical and cognitive delays and/or symptoms. For example, often children with a complex trauma history will struggle to form a healthy attachment in their relationships with others (The National Child Traumatic Stress Network, n.d.). Chloe seemed to respond in this way with her father even in his attempts to keep her safe. Furthermore, children with complex trauma display inappropriate and unpredictable emotional responses (The National Child Traumatic Stress Network, n.d.). Chloe manifested these responses when she discussed her rising anger issues in her pre-teen through her teen years. Finally, complex trauma can cause young people to behave erratically and engage in risky behaviors such as the ones Chloe engaged in through getting pregnant and her actions during her time when she resided with her mother (The National Child Traumatic Stress Network, n.d.).

These effects can act as warning signs for educators. When these signs are detected in students, this is likely the time to take appropriate action. However, what might be the best course of action? Educators should work toward building relationships of trust with students like Chloe. This seems counterintuitive considering the prior research that suggests this would be difficult to do for someone suffering from trauma; however, the same evidence suggests that building relationships is the right starting point.

For example, Chloe mentioned two people in her interview: a school counselor and a detective that built relationships during her struggle that she would hold onto later. She referred to the school counselor as "the educator in my story [who] enters my life when I was about 8 years old. And she would end up being my mentor to this day and she is in her 80s now." She referred to the officer again as someone who was, "the first time during that period of time when somebody looked at me like I was a human." Even though Chloe struggled to reciprocate in those relationships early on while experiencing the effects of trauma, she would later turn to those relationships in her time of need. Especially her incredible father, whom she repeatedly reached out to in her darkest hour. While there will not be much an educator can do or is expected to do, considering their professional expertise or lack thereof in working with students struggling with effects of trauma, the most effective action they can and should take is to continue to build a positive relationship with that student. In fact, an adult's capacity to build positive relationships and environments can improve emotional wellness and reduce stress (Erlauer, 2003).

The brain plays a role in this process as well. Neuroscience research has indicated that the frontal lobes of the brain, the part of the brain that houses most of the brain's executive function such as planning, choices, and decision-making, do not fully develop until a person is in their mid-20s

(Johnson, Blum, & Giedd, 2009). Before that point, decisions are made without a mature capacity to do so. Therefore, the decisions Chloe made, which ultimately led her into being trafficked, were made without a fully matured part of her brain that would allow her to make the best decisions. The good news: this part of the brain can be developed and changed with time and experience (Jensen, 2016; Kolb et al., 2012).

Recall being an adolescent and making an immature decision. What did a parent, guardian, extended family member, peer, and/or teacher/coach/advisor say in response to the decision? In light of neuroscience research, the question "What were you thinking?" often posed by the above-mentioned parties seems comical because the answer provided by neuroscience research, "we weren't!" Therefore, Chamberlin (2009) recommends,

> While part of adolescence is about seeking new experiences and independence, teens still need lots of quality time with healthy adults to help shape their brains and learn the skills to transition into adulthood. They need the guidance of adults' mature prefrontal cortexes, even more so when they have histories of trauma. (p. 2)

Therefore, guiding and mentoring students like Chloe, who were presented with choices from parties who seek to deceive and mislead in their decision-making processes, can be pivotal to positive cognitive development and may help them avoid disastrous and devastating consequences.

CONCLUSION

This chapter began with a bleak outlook of the human-trafficking situation in the United States. Fortunately, victims like Chloe were able to escape the chains of human trafficking, and their stories allow those who work with adolescents to be the difference in curbing these trends. By providing Chloe's narrative, the hope is that educators and others who work with adolescents gain a better understanding of some of the factors that lead individuals into becoming victims of human trafficking. Likewise, educators who apply the strategies of building strong social and emotional relationships with the adolescents may be able to help those individuals self-regulate their emotions and subsequently develop a stronger cognitive capacity to make sound and healthy decisions. In closing, Jensen (2016) said it best, "Shift your mindsets enough to become a seriously powerful change agent and an unstoppable playmaker who makes miraculous events happen every day" (p. 20).

READER TAKEAWAYS

• Human trafficking continues to be a large-scale problem ensnaring young adolescent women across the United States.
• A variety of cognitive, social, emotional, and psychological factors may contribute to a young woman's entanglement into human trafficking.
• Teachers equipped with the knowledge of the aforementioned factors coupled with the capacity to foster caring and positive relationships can help to mitigate further cases of human trafficking among adolescent women.

NOTE

1. See Pimpin, K., & Hunter, K. (2007). *Law five: Prey on the Weak. Pimpology: The 48 laws of the game*. New York, NY: Spotlight Entertainment. Retrieved from https://books.google.com/books?id=p3C6srOcw9IC&printsec=frontcover#v=onepage&q&f=false

REFERENCES

Banks, D., & Kyckkelhahn, T. (2011). *Characteristics of suspected human trafficking incidents, 2008–10*. Washington, DC: U.S. Department of Justice, Office of Justice Programs, Bureau of Justice Statistics. Retrieved from http://www.bjs.gov/content/pub/pdf/cshti0810.pdf

Chamberlain, L. B. (2009). The amazing teen brain: What every child advocate needs to know. *Child Law Practice, 28*(2), 17–24. Retrieved from http://childrenslawoffice.com/wp-content/uploads/2012/02/The-Amazing-Teen-Brain.pdf

Erlauer, L. (2003). *The brain-compatible classroom: Using what we know about learning to improve teaching*. Alexandria, VA: Association for Supervision and Curriculum Development.

Jensen, E. (2016). *Poor students, rich teaching: Mindsets for change*. Bloomington, IN: Solution Tree Press.

Johnson, S. B., Blum, R. W., & Giedd, J. N. (2009). Adolescent maturity and the brain: the promise and pitfalls of neuroscience research in adolescent health policy. *The Journal of Adolescent Health, 45*(3), 216–221. doi:10.1016/j.jadohealth.2009.05.016

Kolb, B., Mychasiuk, R., Muhammad, A., Li, Y., Frost, D. O., & Gibb, R. (2012). Experience and the developing prefrontal cortex. *Proceedings of the National Academy of Sciences of the United States of America, 109*, 17186–17193. doi:10.1073/pnas.1121251109

Monique. (n.d.). Look into my eyes. *MTV U against our will campaign*. Retrieved from http://www.againstourwill.org/survivor-poetry

The Human Trafficking Institute. (2017). *2017 federal human trafficking report.*
    Retrieved from https://www.traffickingmatters.com/wp-content/uploads/2018/05/
    2017-Federal-Human-Trafficking-Report_hi-res.pdf
The National Child Traumatic Stress Network. (n.d.). *What is child trauma?*
    Retrieved from https://www.nctsn.org/what-is-child-trauma
The National Human Trafficking Hotline. (2018). *Hotline statistics.* Retrieved from
    https://humantraffickinghotline.org/states
The U.S. Department of State. (2000). *Victims of trafficking and violence protection act
    of 2000* (Public law 106-386). Retrieved from https://www.state.gov/documents/
    organization/10492.pdf

Chapter 5

The Bully, the Bullied, and the Bystanders

Dana Mayhall, PhD

It is a fundamental democratic right for a child to feel safe in school and to be spared the oppression and repeated, intentional humiliation implied in bullying.

Dan Olweus

Expected Chapter Learning Outcomes:

- Readers will gain understanding of the issue of bullying in public schools through the eyes of a bullying victim.
- Readers will learn prevention and intervention strategies to help educators, parents, and students successfully deal with bullying.

The United Nations Convention on the Rights of the Child states that protection from abuse is imperative for the quality of life every child has a right to expect (United Nations, 1991). However, in our changing society, many children do not have this right due to bullying in public schools. One in every five students report that they have been bullied at school, with 33 percent reporting they had been bullied more than twice in the last month (National Center for Education Statistics [NCES], 2016). It is impossible to completely predict who will be bullied because the bully-victim relationship is "normative"—bullying can happen in any school and among students in all different circumstances (Smith & Brain, 2000).

The definition of what constitutes bullying is debated among professionals and educators. Harris and Petrie summarized it best when they stated that bullying is "intentionally harmful aggressive behavior of a more powerful person or group of people directed repeatedly toward a less powerful person, usually without provocation" (2003, p. 2).

Bullying happens in a variety of ways—physical, verbal, relational, emotional, and, now, cyberbullying through the Internet. A bully may use fear, intimidation, gestures, harassment, threats, humiliation, or social isolation to affect others negatively. This can be done in direct, face-to-face ways, or indirectly through cunning schemes and harassment. If something is not done to intervene, bullying can scar a victim's life and possibly even lead to being "bullied to death" (Miller & Lowen, 2012). Over 50 percent of school-shooting attackers were victims of bullying in school.

Bullying takes place in or near schools where adult supervision is limited or nonexistent—hallway/stairwell (42 percent), classroom (34 percent), cafeteria (22 percent), outside school grounds (19 percent), school bus (10 percent), and bathroom/locker room (9 percent) (NCES, 2016). Bullying is reported more among young adolescents, 10–14 years old, while they are in middle school, but bullying can happen in both elementary and high school. Physical bullying is much higher in younger children, becoming less likely as they age. The opposite is true of cyberbullying incidents—it is seldom seen in younger children, but increases in middle and high school (Harris & Petrie, 2003).

So how does bullying affect children and their education? What about the victim, the bully, and even the bystanders? As you read Craig's story, consider this "bullying triangle" and the trauma this young man endured at the hand of bullies. What should the school have done? In what ways can educators make a difference in this type of behavior?

STUDENT NARRATIVE

Craig's Story

The darkness all started when we moved again to another community. My dad is in the military so we always had to move when he got new orders. It is hard for me to make new friends when we move—maybe because I'm the new kid, but probably because of how I look. My mom says I'm beautiful and sweet, but that doesn't work for a fifth grade boy. Yeah, I guess I've got good looks, but that didn't keep kids from making fun of me.

Mom says I wasn't really a boy's boy, but the kids just called me "gay" or "girlie" or whatever other slam they could think of. I was an easy target for these taunts because I really didn't stand up for myself. I tried to stay to myself and didn't really tell my parents or anyone about the bullying. I just ignored it and hoped it would stop, but it didn't get better.

Once I got to middle school, my parents thought getting into football would be good for me and maybe I could make some friends or things like that. I thought since we were in Texas maybe playing football would help me make friends and be accepted. My seventh grade year was miserable. My team members would make fun of me all the time and I got pushed around in the hallways, too. At first, it wasn't really that bad—I just learned to ignore it.

My parents asked me how it was going so I told them the kids here were a bit meaner than others in the past, but I could handle it. They told me they cared and to let them know if I have problems I can't handle myself. They also told me to tell a teacher if someone is bullying me. I listened, but I wasn't about to tell a teacher. I thought I was strong enough to handle it, but, boy, was I wrong.

The bullying increased more and more, but I didn't say anything. It was almost like the darkness was swallowing me up. My mom asked me about how it was going and I tried to make it seem okay. She asked, "Is this just normal boys teasing each other or is it something more?" I answered, "No, I think it's just more than it should be, but I don't really know." She seemed concerned, but just asked me to keep her posted if it continued or got any worse.

One afternoon during football practice, the guys were making fun of me for being so small and started calling me names again. I tried to ignore them, but it just got worse and worse. Suddenly Derrick, the star linebacker and most popular seventh grade boy, grabbed the back of my football helmet and forced my head down toward my crotch. Everyone laughed as he made fun of me for being gay and "liking it that way." Everybody laughed and laughed. One of the guys tried to get them to stop, but then the coaches blew their whistle and started the drill. I thought the coaches saw what happened without doing anything about it.

I ran home after practice and tried to get upstairs before anyone saw me, but Mom could tell I was devastated when I walked in the house. She got dad and they wanted to know what happened so I told them about what Derrick and the others had done. They were very upset and asked me what I wanted them to do about it. I was afraid for them to do anything because if you address it and it doesn't get handled right, then it just makes it worse. I said, "One of the boys stopped it and the coaches saw it." Mom said, "Okay, so they're gonna handle it?" and I answered, "Yes!"

I believed the coaches would handle it, but it gradually got worse throughout the season. I just played the games and then kept to myself most of the rest of the year. Mom and Dad questioned me about how it was going, and I flat out lied. I told them, "No, it's fine. It was handled. It's not a big deal." They were sort of satisfied even though it was really never handled and just continued to get worse.

The bullying was so bad I decided not to play football in eighth grade. My parents were confused about why I didn't want to play. I didn't tell them that I just didn't want to put myself out there to be attacked again. I tried to stay under the radar, and it worked for a little while. It was only a few months into that year when it started again, but this time it was in choir. This kid in my section kept calling me names and poking at me during practice.

For weeks I tried to ignore him or move away from him, but nothing seemed to work; he just kept going and going. I told the teacher about it so she knew that this kid wouldn't leave me alone. She could have switched our places in the choir, but she continued to put us together. I finally told mom and dad about the kid, and they asked the teacher to do something about it.

Mom also talked to the school counselor who promised mom she'd be keeping an eye on me. The counselor would see me in the hall and ask how I was doing, and all I said was, "OK." What was I going to do—tell her they were doing it again? She was asking me right out there in the hallway where everyone could hear. Even though my parents tried, the school didn't help stop the bullying.

A few weeks later, we had a choir concert and I had to stand in front of this kid again. He poked me in the back over and over again. I tried to ignore it because this concert was our last grade for the semester, but I just couldn't take it anymore. I turned around and yelled at him to stop it. The teacher heard me and I got in big trouble. The one time I stand up for myself, and the adult comes down on me—I nearly failed choir because of that other kid's bullying. I just thought, "Well, crap, I'm not gonna stand up for myself anymore, I'm not gonna do this anymore."

Everything just continued to get worse. My parents tried to talk to the choir teacher again, and she said she'd take care of it, but nothing helped. It became harder and harder to even get out of bed, much less go back to that school where I was bullied every day. I didn't have any help to protect me from those mean kids—no coach or teacher would do anything about it. I had no hope of it ending so I just lost it.

That night I was so depressed and tired of it all, I freaked out. The darkness was winning. I just didn't want to be here anymore so I tied the sheet around my neck and started to hang myself, but something stopped me. I started crying and ran into my parent's bedroom. My mom jumped out of bed and whispered, "Dude, what's wrong? What's going on?" I answered, "Mom, I need you." She said, "Okay, I'm here, I'm here. Let me get my robe and. . .," but I couldn't stop. I ran back into my bedroom and started hyperventilating. I was in a panic.

Mom followed me into my room and I cried out. "I can't do this anymore. I can't go back to that school. I can't. . . . Nobody will do anything, they won't stop, nobody will listen to me. I just can't do it anymore. I can't be here anymore."

Mom answered, "Alright, dude, stop. You have to stop. Breathe. Sit down on the bed and breathe. I'll go get dad and we can sit down and talk." She ran out the door and returned quickly with my dad. They sat down on either side of me on the bed.

Dad said, "Okay, son, talk to us." I started to tell them how desperate I was to end this pain and torment. I reached over and grabbed the knotted sheet. My parents got very upset when they realized I tried to kill myself because I couldn't handle dealing with those kids anymore. I know my parents wanted to help, but every time they tried to talk to a teacher, it didn't do any good—it just made things worse.

Mom and Dad weren't sure what to do so they took me to the emergency room. The nurses and doctors asked me lots of questions. Mom said they were doing an evaluation to see if I needed to go to a treatment center or something. My dad who is ex-military said he thought I had PTSD from all the bullying.

I didn't have to stay in the hospital or anything, but my parents took me to a counselor right away. My mom stayed home with me for a few weeks while I worked with the counselor to try and figure out how to handle the bullies. During this time, I was away from school, my mom met with the school counselor and some teachers to try and get some real help. She told them about what had happened and that things had to change at school.

Mom told them, "Let me tell you, if I have to go through this again, I will not lose my son. I will not. We are damn lucky that we are as close to our son that he was able to tell us what was going on." Mom told the counselor she expected her to meet with me every day to make sure no one was bullying me.

I went back to school and things were okay for a few weeks, but the bullies started in on me again. At first, the counselor would call me in every couple of weeks, but most of the time I just told her, "Nope, I'm good, I'm fine. Whatever." I guess I should have told her it was still happening, but I really didn't think it would help.

There was another big problem with that kid in choir so I told my mom. She called the counselor, who told the principal, and I got called into his office. The principal wanted to know what had happened and who had bullied me. I really am not the kind of guy who tells on people, but this time I thought maybe it would help so I told the principal who was bullying me. He said he'd take care of it, but nothing happened. That kid in choir never got moved or changed classes and he kept picking on me.

My mom asked me how things were going so I told her nothing had changed. She got angry and called the school counselor again. Mom demanded to know what the principal had done about it. The counselor said she wasn't sure what had been done with the boys that had been turned in for bullying me, but she would check with the principal right away.

The next day at school, the principal called me into his office again. He said, "Craig, your mom called and said that you were having another issue in choir. Do you wanna tell me what's going on?" I answered him, "Um, sir, I told you what was going on three weeks ago." And he said, "No, you didn't." And I said, "Yes, sir I did. I even gave you his name." And the principal looked at me and said, "I don't know what you're talking about. No, you didn't."

I was so shocked by what the principal said, but being a respectful kid, I wasn't going to disagree with him. I answered him, "You know what? You're probably right. I'm sorry, my mom must be mistaken. Just drop it and let it go." The principal just told me to go back to class, so I did. I didn't know this at the time, but the counselor called my mom back and told her that I said my mom had made a mistake. Boy, did this make my mom mad! She told the counselor that she was on the way up to school and she needed to have me brought to the office right away.

When mom got to school, she asked me what was going on. She wanted to know if I had told her the truth or made it up that I told the principal the names of the bullies. I told her, "Mom, I went in there. I told that principal who the kids were and exactly what happened. He is calling me a liar and telling me that I didn't do it." Mom was so upset, we went right home and she called my dad. My parents discussed the situation and went back to the school together to meet with the principal.

My dad explained the situation once again and told the principal how I had been bullied for so long at that school. The principal seemed frustrated and asked my dad, "What do you expect me to do about it?" My dad was very angry and responded, "Do your f**king job! That's what I want you to do. That's all I'm asking you to do, do your job. My son came in here and told you exactly what was going on, exactly what happened and you're not willing to do a thing about it."

The principal answered, "Well, I'm not sure Craig told me the names of the boys." The principal stepped out of the office and asked his secretary if I had come in the office." She told the principal that I had come in and that I had given her the names of the bullies. The principal apologized to my parents and told them he'd take care of it . . . yeah, right.

A few days later I was sitting at lunch at a table of guys, some of which were play-slapping each other. The principal stopped by the table and said, "Boys, you better stop that right now, before one of your parents calls me and tells me one of you is being bullied." I told my parents about this and my dad called the principal to ask what he meant by that comment. The principal said he didn't mean it like that, but, really, what could he have meant? He was just being a big bully himself.

I begged my parents to homeschool me for the rest of my eighth-grade year, but my mom was afraid I'd become completely isolated from other kids if she did that. I finished that year by trying to keep to myself and not be a target for anyone.

I'm now in high school and, I guess, the bullying is not as bad here. My parents have advocated with the school district to use a bullying prevention program, and they have slowly started implementing one. But the thing is, those same kids are still in school with me now so I constantly look over my shoulder, afraid the darkness will overwhelm me again.

I never play football anymore and I don't join any other school groups. I keep to myself and get home as soon as I can when I finish classes. I miss that kid I was before all this bullying started, but I don't think I'll ever feel safe enough to be myself again. The darkness is always there, ready to overtake me again.

BRAIN RESEARCH AND LEARNING

In the case of Craig, what could have possibly driven those students to bully him in such damaging ways? Bullies are not always the student who gets in trouble or refuses to do homework. Bullies, like Derrick, may often be popular with other students and teachers, be a good student, and have caring parents. However, most bullies have trouble managing their emotions, are aggressive and confrontational, have little concern or empathy for others, are quick to anger, and know how to use manipulation to get their own way.

Bullies can control others through verbal threats and physical actions, can be antisocial, and are more likely to break school rules than others. Many times, students use bullying because they haven't developed other coping skills to face challenges in life. They are just as at risk of having emotional problems as the children they victimize. Students who are always bullying others can have many problems that follow them into adulthood, such as aggression, alcohol and drug abuse, quick tempers, violent actions, depression, and difficulties with relationships (Carpenter & D'Atona, 2014; Harris & Petrie, 2003; Hazler, Carney, & Granger, 2006; Miller & Lowen, 2012).

Bullied students are not always like Craig, but anyone can be a target of bullying behavior. Victims of bullying may be more passive, anxious, insecure, quiet, or afraid of confrontation. They may also be physically smaller and weaker than other students and have a harder time interacting with their peers. The bullied student may feel socially isolated and have a poor self-concept. Students who are bullied may have difficulty sleeping and experience nightmares, as well as a reduced appetite and trouble learning in school. They may also want to miss school, try to hurt themselves, and even have suicidal thoughts or actions.

Bullying can inhibit academic performance, lower self-esteem, hinder social relationships, encourage dropping out, and cause constant emotional stress. Being a target can lead to hopelessness and have long-term effects. The emotional damage of bullying will last even longer than the physical harm done to the victim. Families of victims have been so desperate to keep their children safe from bullies that they change schools, move to another home, and even move out of town to protect their children (Carpenter & D'Atona, 2014; Harris & Petrie, 2003; Hazler, Carney, & Granger, 2006; Miller & Lowen, 2012).

What about the third party in the bullying triangle—the bystanders? Sometimes bullies like to have an audience because the presence of bystanders can increase the negative impact of the bullying for the victim and can give the bully more power and recognition. Bystanders can be anyone—kids, parents, teachers, adults, bus drivers, lunch aides, principals, and so on. In fact, there are many more bystanders than bullies and victims combined.

But why are the bystanders being passive and doing nothing about the bullying? Many bystanders believe that bullying is funny as evidenced in the various YouTube videos of kids bullying kids. Those who are passively watching the bullying may not know what to do or think that telling someone would not accomplish anything. Others think that if they do something to intervene, the bully may turn on them as the target.

Observing these incidents can bring up conflicting emotions of guilt and fear and increase the bystander's stress and feelings of hopelessness. The onlookers of a bullying incident are generally ignored by the adults and educators of the school, but they need attention as well as the victims and bullies (Harris & Petrie, 2003; Miller & Lowen, 2012).

Researchers have begun to study the effects of bullying behavior on the brain of victims and bullies alike. Emily Anthes, a science writer for *The Boston Globe*, states, "Bullying can leave an indelible imprint on a teen's brain at a time when it is still growing and developing. Being ostracized by one's peers, it seems, can throw adolescent hormones even further out of whack, lead to reduced connectivity in the brain, and even sabotage the growth of new neurons" (Anthes, 2010).

In the human brain, the cortex is in charge of all reasoning and executive functions. The cortex takes in information and tries to make connections between these new data and related material in the brain. This allows the cortex to make reasonable decisions based on prior experience.

The amygdala in the brain, however, determines emotional responses and gets agitated by anything that is different. The cortex communicates with the amygdala to try and justify or even reduce the level of emotional responses. This is because stress, pressure, and trauma can disturb the chemical balance in the brain and overwhelm the amygdala and in turn override the cortex, which leads to impulsivity and misperceptions. Because the brain continues to grow throughout life and the chemical balance is so important to this growth, bullying is a severe form of trauma and must be taken seriously (Anthes, 2010; Sanchez, 2017).

The brain's chemical makeup can be greatly affected by hormones of boys and girls, but in different ways. Boys have testosterone hormones that make males more physically aggressive and with a tendency to become angry. They have a larger amygdala that is responsible for increased competitiveness and impulsive behavior. Therefore, boys are more prone to act out physically and be more involved in physical forms of bullying.

The estrogen found in females is sometimes called the "peace-loving" drug that increases communication and empathy. Their smaller amygdala prevents girls from reaching a level of emotional loss of control that blocks the cortex. Girls aren't as physical when it comes to bullying because they are not driven by the need to be physically impulsive. Girls are more calculating and cunning as they use ostracizing of their victims. This isolating of the bullied student diminishes their self-control and creates feelings of sadness and depression (Anthes, 2010; Sanchez, 2017).

In his book *Bullying and the Brain: Using Cognitive and Emotional Intelligence to Help Kids Cope*, Plaford (2006) shares that current brain research suggests to help students deal with the bullying issue, educators must build the emotional intelligence of their students. He goes on to say that emotional intelligence means to have an understanding of your own emotions and how they affect you. A person with a high emotional intelligence can explain and discuss what they are feeling and understand the thoughts and feelings of others. They are typically not out of control and have a strong sense of empathy.

Social and emotional skills can be learned so that one's emotional intelligence can grow and students can successfully manage their emotions. Teachers need to help their students recognize and deal with emotional triggers, and then come up with the strategies for coping with different events. This can be done through modeling, writing, role playing, discussions, and reading.

Educators need to help their students develop more positive thought habits as well as an outward focus to care about others. Schools that have determined to build the emotional intelligence of the students report that student success has increased and there were decreased incidents of bullying and victimization (Miller & Lowen, 2012; Plaford, 2006; Sanchez, 2017).

In order to uphold the civil rights of all students and provide a safe learning environment, federal, state, and local governments have provided guidelines and requirements for districts to follow in order to stop bullying in schools. There are also many organizations that work to prevent and intervene when bullying takes place. The federal government has established a website (https://www.stopbullying.gov) that provides information for students, parents, and schools as it relates to preventing bullying behaviors.

But what about schools where the bullying takes place? The first step in addressing bullying is not to ignore it. Bullying will not stop on its own and, if it is ignored, it will usually get worse. Schools must admit they have a bullying problem and determine to do something about it (Plaford, 2006). Then schools must establish a safe environment for the students so they won't be afraid to report bullying and to trust that the adults will use effective interventions to stop it if it does happen. If this is not done, students will continue to bully, victims will continue to be hurt, and parents of the victims will get frustrated due to lack of response by school officials.

CONCLUSION

Schools need to establish a culture of openness and support for their students by working with staff, parents, and communities to prevent bullying. Successful prevention involves fostering connections between adults and students to provide a cultural shift of acceptance for all students and zero tolerance for bullying behaviors. Staff development training can provide classroom teachers and other personnel with appropriate strategies to address bullying. Teachers can use social-emotional learning techniques to help shift students' brains from emotional to thoughtful responses and to learn to trust one another.

Through meaningful classroom conversations and activities, teachers can make sure that all parties involved in bullying are addressed. Connections with good role models and building positive relationships can help both the bully and victim to develop healthy self-concepts as well as to learn to interact in healthier ways. Schools need to foster upstanding behavior—the courage and strength to stand up and intervene on behalf of another student instead of just being a bystander. Parents of both victims and bullies must also work in partnership with the school to help their children.

With all these strategies in place, schools can create an inclusive school climate where diversity is welcome and students feel safe and appreciated (Harris & Petrie, 2003; Miller & Lowen, 2012; Plaford, 2006; Sanchez, 2017).

READER TAKEAWAYS

- All students deserve a safe and caring school environment where bullying is not tolerated.
- The stress and trauma of bullying can negatively affect the growing brains of children and lead to lifelong problems.

• Educators and schools must take responsibility to establish a safe place of learning for all students.

REFERENCES

Anthes, E. (2010, November 28). Inside the bullied brain. *The Boston Globe*. Retrieved from http://archive.boston.com/bostonglobe/ideas/articles/2010/11/28/inside_the_bullied_brain

Carpenter, M., & D'Atona, R. (2014). *Bullying solutions: Learn to overcome from real case studies*. Hauppauge, NY: Barron's Educational Series.

Harris, S., & Petrie, G. (2003). *Bullying: The bullies, the victims, the bystanders*. Lanham, MD: Scarecrow Press.

Hazler, R. J., Carney, J. V., & Granger, D. A. (2006). Integrating biological measures into the study of bullying. *Journal of Counseling & Development, 84*(3), 298–307. doi:10.1002/j.1556-6678.2006.tb00409.x

Miller, C., & Lowen, C. (2012). *The essential guide to bullying: Prevention and intervention*. New York, NY: Penguin Group.

National Center for Education Statistics (NCES, 2016). Retrieved May 24, 2019, from https://nces.ed.gov/fastfacts/display.asp?id=719

Olweus, D. (2013). School bullying: Development and some important challenges. *Annual Review of Clinical Psychology, 9*(1), 751–780. doi:10.1146/annurev-clinpsy-050212-185516

Plaford, G. R. (2006). *Bullying and the brain: Using cognitive and emotional intelligence to help kids cope*. Lanham, MD: Rowman & Littlefield.

Sanchez, H. (2017). *The education revolution: How to apply brain science to improve instruction and school climate*. Thousand Oaks, CA: Corwin.

Smith, P. K., & Brain, P. (2000). Bullying in schools: Lessons from two decades of research. *Aggressive Behavior, 26*(1), 1–9. doi:10.1002/(SICI)1098-2337(2000)26:1%3C1::AID-AB1%3E3.0.CO;2-7

United Nations. (1991). *United Nations convention on the rights of the child*. Florence: UNICEF.

Chapter 6

Place-Based Race: Expectations of Discrimination in Public School Settings

Natalie Welcome, PhD

Teaching is repeating until learning takes place.

Michael A. Smith

Expected Chapter Learning Outcomes:

- Readers will explore a series of experiences that have shaped an individual's opinions about racism.
- Readers will observe research that connects to the experiences highlighted in the narrative.
- Readers will be encouraged to consider how institutions and systems can promote racial divisions and how individual choices contribute to participation.

The 2018 U.S. Census Report estimates that about 76 percent of persons living in the United States identify as white/Caucasian, with about 16 percent of that group being of Hispanic or Latino descent (U.S. Census, 2018). This statistic accounts for the majority of the U.S. population. The next largest ethnic groups are Hispanic/Latino and African American/black, at approximately 18 percent and 13 percent, respectively. Meanwhile, you will find that the narrator of this discussion speaks from the perspective of an African American/black person who describes racist affronts allegedly perpetrated by Caucasian/white individuals.

Keep in mind that there is virtually no way to address every complexity of race relations in a book's chapter, so relevant research is narrowly contextualized from an African American/black and Caucasian/white analytical point of view. This limitation is, in no way, intended to disregard the experiences of others or signify one perspective as having greater importance than others.

Instead, readers are encouraged to seek rich insight regarding these circumstances and then relate qualified research to positively inform choices and decision-making in a school setting.

One stipulation our text's narrator mentioned before sharing personal experiences is that no pity is sought or desired. Rather, the narrator seeks to call awareness to issues of racism in schools and hopes to represent how encounters with racist attitudes inevitably shape an individual's mindset.

A TRANSFORMATIVE JOURNEY THROUGH EXPECTATIONS

The System

The first racist encounter I recall happened to me in elementary school, in kindergarten. A classmate and I were arguing over a ball, pulling it back and forth, each wanting it for ourselves. "I had it first!" I said. "No," the white student protested. "I had it first!" Our teacher approached us, two small kids, about the same height, looking up at the leader, pleading our individual cases. Before long, the teacher had reflexively smacked me in the mouth. She regretted it immediately, as I could see it in her face. Her eyes opened widely and she covered her mouth with both hands.

I knew something was wrong about the way that incident had unfolded. My teacher may have apologized, but I mostly remember contempt on her countenance, which morphed into regret following the slap. And then, I remember her being extremely nice to me.

Everyday thereafter, Schoolyard Smacker went out of her way to treat me well. During our classroom Christmas party a couple of months later, the teachers gave every kid in the class a Christmas bag of candy and small toys. Schoolyard Smacker gave me the biggest, best Christmas bag of them all, stuffing mine with more than the rest of the students' bags.

In hindsight and with a developed mind to ponder these things, I believe I was slapped because the teacher saw my blackness. I suppose her personal feelings about race superiority ran so deeply, they drove her to loathe a child. It seems she loathed me so much that she used my disagreement with another student as an opportunity to hit me rather than to teach two impressionable children a much-needed lesson about sharing.

Reminiscing over this experience forced me to think about the way I was and how it would make me a target for maltreatment. As a kindergartener, I lacked the mental development and wherewithal to spot indicators pointing toward racism. However, through continued exposure to similar attitudes and incidents, I learned to expect unwarranted mistreatment from classroom teachers toward non-white students in a public school setting.

In sixth grade, and with a mind barely developed enough to navigate very complex situations, I encountered a physical education teacher who even I, as a teenager, determined to be a radical racist. He was a jokester, though many of his jokes targeted black people. Once, in front of the whole class of students, Radicalized Racist likened the texture of my hair to a brillo pad. Although only "joking," he often warned white students not to get too close to black students in the risk of getting dark. These kinds of things were said and done openly a 1980s North Carolina classroom.

In recent years, I have spoken with two other professionals who worked with Radicalized Racist at the time and they confessed knowledge of his racist ideology. As they confirmed my suspicions about school teachers in general, I could hardly believe my ears, knowing they did nothing to help curtail those crimes. Through continued exposure to similar attitudes and incidents, I learned to expect unbridled taunting from all kinds of teachers toward non-white students in a public school setting.

During my eighth-grade year, a school guidance counselor was brought in to advise my class about what kind of career paths we might consider. I said, "I want to be a lawyer!" I had felt a drive to dress professionally and rightly represent the law since watching courtroom television shows as a small child. Yet, our guidance counselor's negative response to my comment was swift and matter-of-fact. She told me to forget about being a lawyer because it would never happen. She said her son was a lawyer who worked long hours, most weekends, and received low wages.

This counselor went on to say that I did not have what was needed to handle these challenges and recommended I choose something else. Some might say that Certified Counselor was only trying to help me, but I understood that she was using code language to teach me that black people did not have the intellectual capacity to become lawyers. She saw my complexion, hair texture, and the structure of my jaw rather than my grade report, which would have been a better predictor of my likelihood to pursue and achieve a law degree.

Furthermore, in my middle school classes, I was among many black students who did not receive an AG (Academically Gifted) certification, while nearly every white student in the same classroom received that certification. This was confirmed through the class roster, which indicated AG certification with the acronym next to each name. Though I asked many teachers and school leaders about how to get signed up, there was always a reason it could not be done.

Deadlines had passed, paperwork was not yet available, or the counselor was not in the office this week to administer the exam. I had no idea how to sign up for AG certification in the face of this opposition. I had no idea which school leader could be responsible for this prevention. Somehow, the system *had provided white students with connections, information, and tools to access titles that celebrated their achievements. Through continued exposure to similar attitudes and incidents, I learned to expect school leaders to say and do just about anything to thwart the progress of non-white students in a public school setting.*

In high school, just before a Martin Luther King Jr. Day assembly, a memorable majority of white students in our school lined up at the school office to check out because they had a doctor's appointment that day. This mass exodus, however, could not have happened without so many participating parties. The parents, I imagine, recommended that their children check out of school before the start of the assembly. The ailing students agreed to leave school. The classroom teachers granted permission to droves of students who asked to go to the office. The office personnel signed the dismissal paperwork.

Many culprits were involved. The line of students checking out was so long, it still surprises me that none of the adults in the school effectively objected. Where was the principal? Where was the superintendent to follow up on such an egregious offense? Finally, through continued exposure to similar attitudes and incidents, I had learned to expect this treatment from a well-maintained system toward non-white students in a public school setting.

Choosing to attend a historically black university for my higher educational degree programs has been among the best decisions I have ever made. It gave me a chance to experience life in the company of people who were so much like me on the exterior (and culturally) that they would be much less likely to judge me based on my looks.

And then, in this university setting, meeting with black people from all over the country, I discovered a collection of horror stories that spanned far beyond the classroom. We shared experiences of disproportionate wages, unfair followings in retail stores, suspicious traffic stops, hecklings in crowds, questionable housing and employment practices and many other nightmares that have gone largely unexplained in American society.

Years later, while traveling in Hong Kong, my sister and I were accosted by a group of three Chinese police officers who asked to see our passports. We were not engaged in unlawful behavior, but only walking along the sidewalk, looking for a shopping center that had been recommended to us as a popular tourist spot. As the officers reviewed our passports and radioed to their dispatcher for confirmation, I asked why we were being questioned. The lady officer said they always check the credentials of "Negriods." Through continued exposure to similar attitudes and incidents, I learned to expect System to have a far-reaching influence.

These series of encounters (and many others not mentioned) have greatly influenced the person I have become. They created in me a mindset to anticipate racism and a gauge to recognize it, realizing that public schools can be preliminary training grounds. On the job, in a new organization, in a grocery store, in a church, and around the world, I learned to be prepared for the treatment I will receive because of my physical appearance and I find it important to inform others of what to expect.

In my early youth, I believed individuals like Schoolyard Smacker, Radicalized Racist, and Certified Counselor were the sole culprits of this seemingly endless cycle of racism. By adulthood, I had finally realized that System was responsible for every single racist exploit and the individuals who drive System are the faces of perpetuation.

I have discovered that System is sometimes inadvertently established, yet willfully maintained, by individuals who facilitate its functionality. As System sends subliminal, and sometimes explicit, messages through television and media about the superiority of the white race, it is the individuals who choose to nurture or neglect System's needs that make or break its manifestation. Individuals choose aggression toward other races of people and individuals choose to permit those aggressions. It is certainly the individuals who give rise to a system that is monstrous in its dealings and destructive in its tactics.

In a different conversation, I would discuss how a better system, also driven by individuals, has gifted me with opportunities to thrive in my career and have the beautiful family I enjoy today. It is a system that counteracts the damage done by racist aggression and creates outlets for all people to become positive contributors to their communities. It is a system where we are not judged by the "color of our skin, but by the content of our character." It is a system in which I, my family, my friends, and many of my coworkers have chosen to actively and enthusiastically participate.

BRAIN RESEARCH AND LEARNING

Critical Race Theory supposes that white privilege, from a social, economic, and legal position, is an unnatural social construct established and maintained by its benefactors (Curry, 2009). We have seen this reality displayed through the narrator's description of public school experiences, where an effective system was comprised of individual participants. Consequently, we must recognize that this problem of race relations in a public school setting may be a pervasive problem and educators can potentially find themselves needed to make unpopular decisions.

Jessica Halliday Hardie, an Associate Professor of Sociology at Hunter College, examined institutional factors contributing to public school racial tensions in North Carolina and found that systemic inequalities are regularly ignored for the preservation of operational methods. For example, school leaders effectively segregate student populations by facilitating enrollment of "middle-class" white students in academically advanced classes while enrolling "redneck" students, black students, and Hispanic students into regular classes.

Hardie discovered that this segregation by classroom level is plainly visible, although largely ignored by teachers, school administrators, and others who can potentially exact change. In this school system, inherent racism is consistently masked with positive rhetoric used to redefine racism and blame an individual racist. Such actions help maintain institutional structures that perpetuate racist aggression toward ethnic minorities (Hardie, 2013).

Dr. Muhammad Khalifa, an Associate Professor in the University of Minnesota's College of Education and Human Development, found that school administrators actively avoid issues surrounding race relations and strive to preserve practices that promote those very issues. He noted that racialized school suspension gaps, which punish African American/black boys at a rate four times greater than Caucasian/white boys, adversely impact student achievement. While school leaders aim to preserve operational practices, they circumvent issues of racial marginalization, essentially undermining academic objectives (Khalifa, 2015).

Beyond the behaviors of school leaders, community members are sometimes involved in perpetuating separatism. Esther Prins, professor at Penn State College of Education, found that some white families intentionally work toward segregated school settings for their children to avoid black and Hispanic classmates for their students (Prins, 2007).

The Hartford Courant, a major news outlet based in Connecticut, reported that a local zoning commission intentionally approves or denies housing development projects to prevent certain race and income classes from accessing housing in Westport, Connecticut (Thomas, 2019). With housing being inherently connected to schooling, these decisions immediately impact race relations in public schools.

There is no question that many school and community leaders are integral parts of systemic processes that promote racial injustices in public schooling. However, as individuals, we choose how we engage within those systems through focused decision-making. Specifically, participation in racist practices is often a result of the normalization of familiar behaviors where educators must identify their sentiments about the norms.

In *Seeing the Strange in the Familiar*, a case study regarding racial practices in public schools, researchers suggest that educators be on the lookout for strange elements of familiar behaviors to constantly advocate for new ways of thinking about common, yet detrimental, practices (Brown, 2010).

CONCLUSION

Research has shown that many racial injustices within public school settings are substantiated and advanced through normalization. Normal behaviors are acceptable because those behaviors are normal. Meanwhile, even well-intentioned school leaders unwittingly become a part of a public school culture characterized by racism simply because cultural practices are common.

For educational leaders who may encounter even the smallest modicum of ethnic diversity in the classroom, participation in race relations must be intentionally considered. As ignoring difficult issues of race relations can be a form of contributing to destructive practices, acknowledging and dismantling those practices can be the start of real change.

READER TAKEAWAYS

- Brain research confirms that racist experiences often impact the victims over extended periods of time and are largely ignored by school and community leaders.
- As an educator of whatever sort, you must choose to support a system where racism is regularly manifested or choose not to support such a system.

REFERENCES

Brown, S., Souto-Manning, M., & Laman, T. T. (2010). Seeing the strange in the familiar: Unpacking racialized practices in early childhood settings. *Race Ethnicity and Education, 13*(4), 513–532.

Curry, T. (2009). Critical race theory. In H. Taylor Greene (Ed.), *Encyclopedia of Race and Crime* (pp. 166–169). Sage.

Hardie, J. H., & Tyson, K. (2012). Other people's racism. *Sociology of Education, 86*(1), 83–102.

Khalifa, M. A., & Briscoe, F. M. (2014, November 30). *A counternarrative autoethnography exploring school districts' role in reproducing racism: Willful blindness to racial inequities*. Retrieved from https://eric.ed.gov/?id=EJ1063217

Prins, E. (2007). Interdistrict transfers, Latino/White school segregation, and institutional racism in a Small California Town. *Journal of Latinos and Education, 6*(4), 285–308.

Thomas, J. R. (2019, May 24). *Separated by design: How some of America's richest towns fight affordable housing*. Retrieved from https://www.propublica.org/article/how-some-of-americas-richest-towns-fight-affordable-housing

U.S. Census Bureau. (n.d.) QuickFacts: United States. Retrieved from https://www.census.gov/quickfacts/fact/table/US/PST045218

Chapter 7

Did You Just Assume My Gender?

Jon McFarland, EdD, and Heidi Kuehn,
Doctoral Candidate

So many assume, so little know.

Anonymous

Expected Chapter Learning Outcomes:

- Readers will gain insight into one transgender student's experiences in high school shared through a personal essay.
- Readers will learn about associated brain research and pedagogical recommendations that promote a culture of care, which can be applied to addressing the needs of LGBTQ+ (Lesbian, Gay, Bisexual, Transgender, Queer) students.

It is the first day of the new school year, and your high school students start to filter into the classroom. You have never had these students before, and as the thirtyish unfamiliar faces file in, you think about learning new names and setting the tone. You want the school year to start off on the right foot. As the tardy bell rings, a palpable sense of both nervousness and excitement spread throughout the room as students settle into their seats. First-day faces look at you, hushing each other, and it begins. You introduce yourself briefly, announcing the name of the course, and the students wait for what comes next. Everyone is a bit unsure of themselves on the first day, but as a teacher, you try to demonstrate a sense of calm and assurance.

You pull out the class roster to take attendance, announcing that you will do your best with the pronunciations. You request students to repeat their names back to you, adding a nickname request if they desire. You cannot help but wonder who all these people are. As you work your way down the list, you encounter "Kylie Newsome." Feeling relief at a name which seems easy to pronounce, you are startled when the student answers, "Jacob Newsome." You check your roster and blurt out, "Do you have a sister in this class, too?" Tension fills the room before Jacob answers meekly, "No." You realize suddenly that you have unintentionally assumed Jacob's gender, and you have just called attention to a name which causes Jacob discomfort.

Assuming gender based on first impressions and societal stereotypes which impact how we perceive others has been a long-held habit for many people (Butler, 1990). In the United States, people have generally assumed that gender is predictably tied to a fixed binary system based on an individuals' sex assigned at birth (Nicolazzo, 2017). In reality, gender is a social construct, developing over time and through interactions with others. It reflects a complexity transcending a male and female binary (Butler, 1990). Some individuals in society resist the idea that gender identity can exist separately from sex assigned at birth which Nicolazzo (2017) termed *compulsory heterogenderism*. This resistance limits our ability to perceive gender identity other than in a normative way. We offer this narrative from Zachary, a transgender student who struggled with gender assumptions in high school.

STUDENT NARRATIVE

In This I Believe: We Are More Than the Sum of Our Parts

"Did you just assume my gender?" That was the meme that haunted my last two years of high school. It's not that I don't have a sense of humor—jokes just aren't funny when your identity is the punch line.

I lived the first seventeen years of my life being shoved into a box that was too small for me. Once I was forced into that box, I was taken and placed in the deepest corner of the closet. From that, I can easily say it is impossible to live happily when you are never set free from [the] walls of your closet. We are more than the sum of our parts and all identities deserve to be respected and taken seriously.

Gender, as a concept, never made sense to me, but I was never really sure why. Growing up I never understood why I had to wear dresses, even though I cried every single time I was forced into one, while my brother was allowed to wear whatever pleased him. The first time I questioned the double standard aloud the response I received was a quick "because you're a girl and he is a boy." From that moment on, I found myself in a constant battle trying to wrap my mind around the concept of gender. At six years old I didn't understand why the body you were born into had to dictate the type of clothes you wore, or the toys you were allowed to play with, or how long your hair was.

Being trans was never anything more than a joke in the small community I grew up in. Slurs and derogatory terms such as "tranny, she-male, he-she, it" and so many others were thrown around my household just as commonly as any other word. Naturally, this led me to believe trans people were nothing more than a joke, so I did what I thought was the right thing to do. I stayed away from the "trannies" and "dressed like a lady."

That was normal for me until I got into high school. For some reason that I didn't understand, being called a girl made my stomach churn with anxiety. I had just convinced my mom to let me cut off all my hair the summer before and I loved it, but I was terrified. "Was my long hair the only thing keeping me a girl?" was something I thought often. I would look in the mirror and repeatedly tell myself I'm a girl and there is nothing I can do about it because that's just the way it is, but I would always end up in tears, wishing that I was something else. That eventually led to me avoiding looking in mirrors altogether because no matter how hard I tried, the reflection was never somebody I enjoyed seeing. This was a particularly difficult time in my young life. One side of me wanted to fight the urges to be the "other." While the opposite side of me wanted to be true to myself and just ditch gender altogether. My conscience was in a constant state of war yet stuck in a standstill.

It wasn't until I met my friend Alicia that I was really okay with my gender identity. I explained to her how I was feeling and what was going through my mind. I will never forget her response, "Dude! You have no gender! Only a fender" (fender because I brought my fender acoustic to school every single day of freshman year). That was the first time anybody told me being "other" was okay. That was also the first time I had a conversation about gender without genitals being mentioned once. That was just the beginning. As my high school years progressed, I became more aware and comfortable with my own identity. However, as my confidence grew so did my awareness of how often non-binary people are used as a joke in my community and media alike. People I went to school with laughed at the idea of an "other" gender. Popular movies and TV shows, such as Zoolander, Deadpool, RuPaul's Drag Race, *and* Hangover *were favorites within my community and unfortunately all use transgender or genderqueer identities for humor.*

I spent seventeen years living in a closet because I was too afraid of what would happen if I tried to leave. I knew if I tried to explain my gender to the people within my community, I would be laughed at because that is what we are taught to do. We are taught that we are born either a boy or a girl and anybody who identifies outside of that binary is either abnormal or "just making it up." Nonbinary genders are obsolete except for when people run out of things to make fun of, which makes it difficult for us to come out and more often than not, those who do come out are met with criticism.

It saddens me that there are people who have to live their whole life in a box. I do want to recognize how lucky I am to be out now, but I am aware of how much work this society needs. I am a strong believer in the idea that gender is just a societal construct and should not be forced onto anybody. All gender identities and expressions are valid and deserve to be respected. I also believe that the sooner we start respecting people for who they are instead of focusing on what anatomy they were born with, the better off the world will be. To put it simply, we are more than the sum of our parts and I cannot wait until the day where people are judged by the content of their hearts instead of the contents of their pants.

BRAIN RESEARCH AND LEARNING

Zachary originally wrote the above essay for a college ethics class. Zachary identifies as transgender (also *trans*), and uses the pronouns "they, them, their." These pronouns can present a challenge for individuals in society who struggle to understand that gender identity can transcend the traditional binaries of "female" and "male." Sometimes, these individuals explain that a lack of familiarity with LGBTQ+ (lesbian, gay, bisexual, transgender, queer/questioning) terminology gets in the way of using correct pronouns and terms (Brauer, 2017). In fact, the problem may go deeper; the pressure to maintain a gender binary is a significant deterrent to learning new words (Nicolazzo, 2017). Both Zachary's account and the anecdote at the beginning of this chapter demonstrate how this lack of knowledge, even when unintentional, can lead to discomfort in the school environment.

Learning how to interact with an increasingly diverse student demographic is fundamental to creating an inclusive environment that demonstrates honor and respect for all individuals. In the classroom, establishing and maintaining such a climate derives, in large part, from the educators' mindset. Zachary's written account describes their experiences in high school and underscores the importance of culturally responsive pedagogical practices. These practices support all students, but especially those who have been historically marginalized (Tillman & Scheurich, 2013). Ideally, all educational institutions would adopt inclusive policies and practices, implementing a *culture of care* in the classroom.

Zachary described being haunted by the question, "Did you just assume my gender?" This likely resonates with trans youth who have had similar experiences both in and outside of the school setting. *Misgendering* is either knowingly or unknowingly assigning the wrong gender identity to an individual, and it is common in schools (Erickson-Schroth & Jacobs, 2017; Kosciw et al., 2018). It occurs more frequently when teachers, administrators, school staff, and even students' peers fail to acknowledge, and even disregard, LGBTQ+ identities (Ansara & Hegarty, 2011). Interactions with individuals based on social norms and stereotypes based on traits, behaviors, and appearances negate and invalidate these identities. Remaining entrenched in normative expectations interferes with developing a deeper understanding and appreciation of sexual orientation, gender identity, and gender expression.

Social justice researchers aim to acknowledge and advocate for historically marginalized groups such as the LGBTQ+ community. *Self-determination*, which describes individuals and groups' rights to control the terms, names, and pronouns used to describe them, is a key component of social justice (Brauer, 2017; Burdge, 2007; Nicolazzo, 2017). In Zachary's case, not only did teachers and peers fail to use the correct pronouns, they also persisted in using Zachary's birth name. This is called *deadnaming*, and, according to students like Zachary, it inflicts pain and can make them feel as if they do not exist.

Zachary described their experiences as "being shoved into a box that was too small" for them. For example, when teachers divide students into groups of "boys" and "girls," this disregards the LGBTQ+ student population and limits the teachers' ability to establish positive relationships with and between all students. It can cause a negative transmission of affect, resulting in tension and discomfort, and ultimately interferes with learning (Brauer, 2017; Jensen, 2016). In Zachary's case, being persistently *misgendered* and *deadnamed* negatively impacted their educational experiences. Zachary's experiences did not reflect a *culture of care*.

Teachers have explained that feeling uncomfortable with LGBTQ+ themes and terminology limits their ability to respond appropriately to name and pronoun requests (Brauer, 2017; Kim, 2009). This discomfort, however, does not absolve teachers from the responsibility of learning how to interact with students such as Zachary. Respecting and honoring all students is a critical component of both inclusive pedagogy and a *culture of care*. Learning how to communicate intentionally and appropriately is fundamental to this type of pedagogy, and there is a growing body of research that supports the creation of professional development programs which would help all educational stakeholders improve in this area.

It seems unlikely that educators would intentionally cause any student harm in the school environment. According to the U.S. Department of Education, Title IX stipulates that no person should be "subjected to discrimination under any education program or activity receiving federal financial assistance" (United States Department of Education [USDOE], 2015). Most schools and school districts have responded to Title IX policies by publishing mission and value statements that profess a commitment to safe and inclusive educational experiences for all students.

Research, however, suggests that these statements do not guarantee that all or even many LGBTQ+ youth experience a safe and welcoming educational environment (Arriaga & Lindsey, 2016; Bustamante, Nelson, & Onwuegbuzie, 2009; Kosciw et al., 2018; Sautner, 2008). The 2017 National School Climate Survey (NSCS) concluded that 99 percent of the LGBTQ+ respondents had heard negative comments about sexual orientation and gender identity at school. The majority of these students also reported that they felt unsafe in that environment due to their sexual orientation, gender identity, or gender expression (California Department of Education, 2019; Kosciw et al., 2018).

Instead of feeling safe and included, surveys like the NSCS indicate that LGBTQ+ youth perceive the school climate as hostile. This climate includes not only peer victimization, but also discriminatory policies and practices as well as homophobic or transphobic comments from teachers and school staff (California Department of Education, 2019; Kosciw et al., 2018). Unsurprisingly, LGBTQ+ students frequently miss school, have lower grade point averages (GPAs), and are less likely to finish high school, let alone pursue higher education (Kosciw et al., 2018). Overall, sexual minority youth (SMY) report lower levels of mental well-being than their non-LGBTQ+ peers (Centers for Disease Control, 2019).

According to the United States Transgender Survey (USTS), trans students experience even higher levels of discrimination than their LGB peers, and this increases even further when their gender identity is known or suspected (James et al., 2016). It is likely that mistreatment in school worsens trans individuals' overall well-being, which may help explain why their attempted suicide rate (40 percent) is nine times that of the general population (James et al., 2016). It is difficult to imagine how students like Zachary manage to navigate such a hostile school climate.

Many LGBTQ+ adolescents in the United States suppress their feelings of otherness to assimilate to a dominantly cis- and heteronormative society. These youth report an exacerbation of internal shame because of the dissonance between their feelings and the hostility they experience with respect to gender and sexuality (Turner & Stets, 2006). Zachary explained that "jokes just aren't funny when your identity is the punch line." When the school environment fails to challenge the proliferation of continually harmful rhetoric and tasteless humor, this directly conflicts with schools' claims that they embrace diversity and support all students. Creating a *culture of care* will allow educators to practice what they preach.

IMPLICATIONS FOR EDUCATORS

Brick-and-mortar public education in the United States is a social engagement deeply rooted in human connection. It is imperative that educators approach student interactions with a relational mindset grounded in empathy. Simply gaining an appreciation for the power of a positive, welcoming, and safe classroom climate is an important first step. Next, educators can begin the process of building an inclusive environment by examining their own implicit biases, which are defined as unconscious and unintentional judgments and motives (Greenwald & Krieger, 2006). Both the anecdote and Zachary's essay reveal the power of biases and assumptions, even when they are unintentional. Valuing human connections, nurturing empathy, confronting biases, and learning about diversity are the foundations of establishing cultural proficiency (Arriaga & Lindsey, 2016) and at the root of creating a *culture of care.*

Research has shown that positive relationships between LGBTQ+ youth and adults in the school environment noticeably increase students' academic success and well-being (Kosciw, Bartkiewicz, & Greytak, 2012). Even one reliable adult ally or advocate can make a big difference. This is not surprising, given the psychological and physiological effect that emotions can have on others (Turner & Stets, 2006). Teachers can have a powerfully positive impact on LGBTQ+ students, just by interacting and communicating with kindness and respect (Brauer, 2017). A *culture of care* decreases students' stress and allows the brain to function better, improving the capacity to learn (Jensen, 2016).

Educators must intentionally generate the discourse, rhetoric, and tone in the classroom setting to promote a positive school climate. Brennan (2004) describes how the diffusion of emotions can affect the social, emotional, and behavioral (re)actions of others. Words are a fundamental aspect of these emotions, and harmful rhetoric can undermine a positive social- emotional learning environment. Zachary experienced hurtful words and sentiments, both in school and at home, and these negative memories increased their anxiety, lowered their self-esteem, and inspired an uncertainty of their place in society. Unfortunately, Zachary's experiences are commonplace for LGBTQ+ youth.

Inclusive pedagogy, policies, and practices support a positive school climate for all students. While "meaningful community building" depends on making "learning personal and purposeful for students" (Goralnik, Millenbah, Nelson, & Thorp, 2012, p. 418), educators must establish the cultural foundation based on inclusivity and respect for all stakeholders. Adopting and implementing a *culture of care* rooted in compassionate and culturally responsive teaching practices paves the way toward improved educational equity for the LGBTQ+ student demographic.

School climate and culture are interrelated. Jensen (2016) explains that "climate" is a broad term, describing the overall feel of the educational environment. School culture is more personal and derives from attitudes and actions of all stakeholders in education. Both school climate and culture are reflected in the enacted policies and practices at educational institutions. LGBTQ+ students are more likely to experience a positive school climate when the culture reflects inclusivity, truly embracing rather than simply tolerating diversity.

Creating a Culture of Care

There are several steps which educators can take to create a *culture of care* for their schools and the diverse students they serve. While there are many more ways to implementing a *culture of care* to support LGBTQ+ students, we highlight some of the most important considerations for educators in getting started.

Be informed

For educators to make a positive impact on their LGBTQ+ students, they must be knowledgeable of the terminology surrounding LGBTQ+ issues. When properly informed of such terms, educators will be adequately equipped to address all stakeholders (i.e., students, parents, administrators, teachers, community advocates) about LGBTQ+ subject matter in and out of the classroom. Furthermore, educators need to understand that gender identity and expression are complex, multifaceted, and nonbinary constructs. For future reference on LGBTQ+ terminology, educators can turn to the ongoing work of the It Gets Better Project or Lambda Legal (It Gets Better Project, 2010; Lambda Legal, n.d.).

Show care with visuals

A great way for educators to demonstrate inclusivity in their classrooms, halls, and offices is with culturally responsive realia in the forms of posters, stickers, or affirmations that promote equality, equity, and acceptance for all individuals regardless of sex, gender identity, or gender expression. Such supplemental material can help demonstrate a safe(r) space for LGBTQ+ youth where they are welcome and protected. Educators can find and invest in such inclusive material through organizations such as the Safe Schools Coalition, the Gilbert Centre, or the National Association of School Psychologists.

Watch your pronouns

A personal sign of recognition for LGBTQ+ youth is to find out students' preferred pronouns and use them faithfully when speaking to and about them, even when they are not present. The overt misuse of gender pronouns is a clear sign of disrespect for trans and other students of self-identified gender. It may be somewhat confusing for educators to use students' preferred pronouns as it requires intentional thought and language use. If educators do happen to accidentally misuse pronouns, it is important to excuse and correct themselves in conversation and communication.

Learn to accept

Teach students' acceptance over tolerance. LGBTQ+ students are part of a diverse group of individuals whose identities are intricate and real. They need our compassion, understanding, and care in order for them to thrive in all aspects of their lives (i.e., academically, socially, emotionally, and psychologically). Tolerance does not promote compassion or equality for LGBTQ+ students when it is not authentic. This may not come easy for some educators, yet promoting an inclusive and positive school culture depends on the educators who play such a vital role in education.

Become an ally

To be an ally for LGBTQ+ individuals is to advocate for them when verbal, physical, or emotional disparities arise. As allies, educators implement culturally responsive practices in and out of the classroom, uphold policies on the use of inclusive language, and enforce policies that protect LGBTQ+ youth from discrimination and harassment.

CONCLUSION

Zachary concludes that "we are more than the sum of our parts." When educators center their interactions with students around empathy, caring, and kindness, the human connection eclipses everything else. As we have seen above, establishing an inclusive school environment for our marginalized LGBTQ+ students takes effort and intentionality from educators. However, the bountiful rewards that result from this effort may include improved citizenship and greater collegiality among all educational stakeholders. Once a *culture of care* has been established in the classroom, the doors to diversity open up, and individuality can blossom.

READER TAKEAWAYS

• Establishing an inclusive and welcoming class environment where all students are comfortable starts with you, the teacher.
• Five easy steps to creating a *culture of care* include being informed about LGBTQ+ issues, posting inclusive visual realia in the classroom, using

appropriate pronouns with LGBTQ+ students, teaching acceptance over tolerance, and becoming an ally.

REFERENCES

Ansara, Y. G., & Hegarty, P. (2011). Cisgenderism in psychology: Pathologizing and misgendering children from 1999 to 2008. *Psychology & Sexuality, iFirst*, 1–24. doi:10.1080/19419899.2011.576696.

Arriaga, T. T. & Lindsey R. B. (2016). *Opening doors: An implementation template for cultural proficiency*. Thousand Oaks, CA: Corwin.

Brauer, D. (2017). *Hiding in plain sight: How binary gender assumptions complicate efforts to meet transgender students' name and pronoun needs* (Doctoral dissertation). Retrieved from https://scholarworks.uvm.edu/cgi/viewcontent.cgi?article=1715&context=graddis

Brennan, T. (2004). *The transmission of affect*. Ithaca, NY: Cornell University Press.

Burdge, B. J. (2007). Bending gender, ending gender: Theoretical foundations for social work practice with the transgender community. *Social Work, 52*(3), 243–250.

Bustamante, R. M., Nelson, J. A., & Onwuegbuzie, A. J. (2009). Assessing school-wide cultural competence: Implications for school leadership preparation. *Educational Administration Quarterly, 45*(5), 793–827.

Butler, J. (1990). *Gender trouble: Feminism and the subversion of identity*. New York, NY: Routledge.

California Department of Education. (2018). *California healthy kids survey*. Retrieved from https://data.calschls.org/resources/Biennial_State_1517.pdf

California Department of Education. (2019). *CalSchls data dashboard*. Retrieved from https://calschls.org/reports-data/dashboard/

Centers for Disease Control (2019). *Youth risk behavior survey: Data summary and trends report, 2007–2017*. Retrieved from https://www.cdc.gov/healthyyouth/data/yrbs/pdf/trendsreport.pdf

Erickson-Schroth, L., Jacobs, L. A. (2017). *"You're in the wrong bathroom!": And 20 other myths and misconceptions about transgender and gender-nonconforming people*. Boston, MA: Beacon Press.

Goralnik, L., Millenbah, K. F., Nelson, M. P., & Thorp, L. (2012). An environmental pedagogy of care: Emotion, relationships, and experience in higher education ethics learning. *Journal of Experiential Education, 35*(3), 412–428.

Greenwald, A. G., & Krieger, L. H. (2006). Implicit bias: Scientific foundations. *California Law Review, 94*(4), 945–967.

Hughes-Hassell, S., Overberg, E., & Harris, S. (2013). Lesbian, gay, bisexual, transgender, and questioning (LGBTQ)-themed literature for teens: Are school libraries providing adequate collections? *School Library Research, 16*, 1–18.

It Gets Better Project. (2010). LGBTQ+ Glossary. Retrieved from https://itgetsbetter.org/lesson/glossary/?gclid=CjwKCAjwzPXlBRAjEiwAj_XTEXgOH_d04PfWQz9SAm6cbfKYr8-xvfhURK7NYdwkoZH5mobM2fJebxoCp-MQAvD_BwE

James, S. E., Herman, J. L., Rankin, S., Keisling, M., Mottet, L., & Anafi, M. (2016). *The report of the 2015 U.S. transgender survey.* Washington, DC: National Center for Transgender Equality.

Jensen, E. (2016). *Poor students, rich teaching: Mindsets for change.* Bloomington, IN: Solution Tree Press.

Kim, R. (2009). *A report on the status of gay, lesbian, bisexual and transgender people in education: Stepping out of the closet, into the light.* Washington, DC: National Education Association.

Kosciw, J. G., Bartkiewicz, M., & Greytak, E. A. (2012). Promising strategies for prevention of the bullying of lesbian, gay, bisexual, and transgender youth. *Prevention Researcher, 19*(3), 10–13.

Kosciw, J. G., Greytak, E. A., Zongrone, A. D., Clark, C. M., & Truong, N. L. (2018). *The 2017 national school climate survey: The experiences of lesbian, gay, bisexual, transgender, and queer youth in our nation's schools.* New York, NY: GLSEN. Retrieved from https://www.glsen.org/sites/default/files/GLSEN-2017-National-School-Climate-Survey-NSCS-Full-Report.pdf

Lambda Legal (n.d.). *Glossary of LGBTQ terms.* Retrieved from https://www.lambdalegal.org/know-your-rights/article/youth-glossary-lgbtq-terms?gclid=CjwKCA jwzPXlBRAjEiwAj_XTESQakrnnaNIgJbe7i2O12RzfF2W9V6tDd8yu19ArCi-JmBW5RX4GxfRoCNAIQAvD_BwE

Nicolazzo, Z. (2017). Compulsory heterogenderism: A collective case study. *NASPA Journal about Women in Higher Education, 10*(3), 245–261.

Sautner, B. (2008). Inclusive, safe and caring schools: Connecting factors. *Developmental Disabilities Bulletin, 36,* 135–167.

Tillman, L. C., & Scheurich, J. J. (2013). *Handbook of research on educational leadership for equity and diversity.* New York, NY: Routledge.

Turner, J. H., & Stets, J. E. (2006). Sociological theories of human emotions. *Annual Review of Sociology, 32,* 25–52.

United States Department of Education. (USDOE, 2015). *Title IX and sex discrimination.* Office of Civil Rights. Retrieved from https://www2.ed.gov/about/offices/list/ocr/docs/tix_dis.html

Chapter 8

"I Just Want to Succeed": The Challenges Faced by Chronically Ill Students

Amber E. Wagnon, PhD

> Understanding the educational needs of students with chronic illness is essential if we are to provide equitable educational opportunities for them.
>
> Shiona Shiu

Expected Chapter Learning Outcomes:

- Readers will gain insight into the experiences of a college student who was diagnosed with Postural Orthostatic Tachycardia Syndrome (POTS) as a teenager.
- Readers will be provided with brain research that connects the experiences of chronically ill students.

Sierra causally stayed after class following our first course meeting. She was enrolled in my college composition course for the sixteen-week-long semester and she wanted to explain to me that sometimes "I pass out." I had never been the teacher of record of a student with a chronic illness. Quite simply, I was not prepared for the reality of her illness.

In hindsight, I should have been prepared for Sierra and other students who experience chronic illness. It is estimated that 17 percent of all students under age 18 suffer from a chronic illness that impacts, at varying levels, their performance in school (Cox, Halloran, Homan, Welliver, & Mager, 2008). This means that educators are likely to work alongside these students on a daily basis.

Consider the story that follows, recounted by Sierra, now in her fourth year of college. In her narrative, Sierra explains how her chronic illness, Postural Orthostatic Tachycardia Syndrome (POTS), impacted her life and her education. As you read, consider: In what ways can educators support students who face chronic illness? How can educators seek to understand the challenges these students face?

STUDENT NARRATIVE

Sierra's Journey

After doing a presentation my sophomore year in high school, I got extremely sick. I was nauseous, dizzy, and my vision became blurry. A few moments later, I fainted. My parents rushed me to the emergency room, where they ran multiple tests on me, and all of the results came back negative. They brushed it off, and said I needed to eat more at breakfast time. I continued on with life, until I passed out again, my junior year. They, again rushed me to the emergency room, and all tests came back negative.

This pattern continued, slowly getting worse. I would pass out once a month, then a few times a month, then once a week, a few times a week. . . . By the time I got to my senior year in high school I was pulled out of all of my sports (basketball, cross country, and track) and passing out two to three times a day. I was only staying unconscious for four up to five minutes at a time. My life did a complete 180.

I went from a top athlete in the top ten percent of my class to a student who could barely pass any of her classes. In the event that I passed out more than three times at school, my school would call my mother, and tell her that I had to go home, even if I felt that I could finish the day. This caused me to miss most of my senior year.

We visited multiple doctors, racking up tons of doctor bills. They always drug tested me, or thought that I had made it all up. My mother ended up quitting her job that same year, because her boss told her she could no longer leave work in the event that I pass out. She became my voice whenever a doctor would brush me off.

We eventually came across a doctor referred to us by a friend, Dr. Amar Suleman, a cardiologist who also lived in Dallas, Texas. When we met him, both my mom and I were extremely tired, and fed up. Mom told him in tears that she just wanted some answers, and he was able to give us just that. I was diagnosed with Postural Orthostatic Tachycardia Syndrome (POTS).

This chronic illness was the cause of me passing out, and a lot of other symptoms I was living with day to day. During a regular day, I was experiencing: headaches, nausea, dizziness, fainting, tachycardia, fatigue, anxiety, mood swings, brain fog, and excessive sweating. I felt all of these symptoms every single day, and most of the symptoms I thought were normal.

Dr. Suleman, a POTS specialist, referred me to his apprentice (another POTS specialist) Dr. Mary Kydrianou (Dr. K). My mother and I were extremely hopeful, because we not only had a diagnosis, but a doctor who seemed determined to fix me. Eventually my POTS got so bad that I was pulled out of school (so I could be less of a distraction to the other students) and home schooled. I went to see Dr. Suleman and Dr. K daily. They worked closely with me, but no results were being seen. I was put on multiple different medications, none of which helped with any of my symptoms.

By August of 2015, I was packed and ready to go to college 3½ hours away from home. I was still passing out, and there were no improvements. As you can imagine, my mom was a nervous wreck, but she sent me away with one of my best friends from high school, Sydney and my boyfriend of a year, Da'Montae. I started college bright eyed, and excited as every freshman should, but things quickly took a turn for the worst.

I was passing out more and more. With every fainting episode my friends, teachers, and the University Police Department would cover me in ice trying to wake me up from my episode. The day came when I was in a criminal justice course and I didn't wake up for an entire hour. *I woke up confused with my teacher sitting beside me and an empty classroom. When I asked where everyone was she'd informed me that I had been out for the whole class, and she sent everyone home early.*

I called and told my mom who burst into tears, and demanded that I come home immediately. She told me that I needed to pack, and she would be there that weekend. I outright refused, and told my mom there was no way I was coming home. We argued, fussed, and fought about it my entire freshman year, but in the end she relented, because I was already a legal adult. She always told me that she would support me in all my decisions, and when I told her that I needed a break from school, that's when she would know that I was tired.

My freshman year was spent crying in my room, watching all of my friends go out and party, because my mom drew the line at parties. She was terrified that I would pass out and be raped, without my friends noticing. I fought her just as hard with the "no party rule" but by the time the argument was over, I would be sick from the fighting and in no condition to go out. I hung out with my boyfriend and watched Grey's Anatomy *the entire semester.*

By the time I got to my sophomore year we all had a good routine down. I would tell my teachers about my illness on the first day of school (something I failed to do as a freshman). I gave them a list of my emergency contacts, and told them not to call unless it had been over fifteen minutes. By this time, the University Police Department was familiar with me and my illness, and if they got there before Da'montae (my boyfriend of two years at this point), they'd call him themselves.

I partied hard, and drank even harder. I had my routine down, and I made up for the lack of partying my freshman year. My friends knew what to do if I passed out, and we went out every weekend, drinking and partying. I stayed in the library with my friends during the week, and studied hard with them. I felt like an unstoppable force by that time. I was excelling in my classes, and I even had a social life.

However, by the time junior year came I was even sicker. I could no longer go out with my friends. I was diagnosed with anxiety and depression, and every summer my POTS doctors would talk about some new and huge break-through they had with POTS patients. Yet, none of them were helpful to me. The few parties I went to made me extremely sick, and drinking didn't help. I was back to square one. I wasn't partying or drinking. I was sitting in my room all day, but this year came with a new hurdle, chronic pain.

My chronic pain became so bad that there were days that I could not get out of bed. The days that I was able to get out of bed, I would go to class and pass out for hours. My work became sloppier and was turned in later. I would stay asleep for eighteen to nineteen hours a day. My teachers would accom-modate me with extra time on assignments, and excused absences but there was only so much they could do. The spring semester I hit rock bottom, and took withheld grades for all of my classes. I had accepted the fact that I would not graduate on time. I was only focused on making it one day at a time.

My senior year hit harder than my junior year. I was only making it to class once or twice a week. My assignments were beyond late, and I was sleeping (unable to be woken up) most of the days away. If I went to class, nine times out of ten I was passed out and unresponsive.

There was nothing anyone could do to help me. My mom and boyfriend tried to keep me motivated, but even that only went so far. I stayed in my room, not even getting out to go to the dining halls. I could not stay awake, and I was in excruciating pain 24/7. There was nothing any of my doctors could give me due to their fear of my depression.

My teachers tried to help by giving me unlimited time on assignments, but I was unable to complete them because I was always unconscious. I felt like a zombie. My brain felt like complete mush, and I was unable to focus on anything. My friends would invite me to events, and they always got the same answer "I don't feel good." I was isolated from everyone except for my boyfriend. I would spend days in my room without leaving before he would get my wheelchair and force me outside to get some sun.

The day came where the university's disability services called me in for a meeting. The semester was almost over. I'd missed most of my classes, barely turned in any assignments. Things were not looking good. My teachers were worried. After a tearful conversation with the head of disability services and my mom, it was determined that I would do a medical withdrawal for the semester. There was no way I could finish the semester. I cried for days, and apologized to my mom for failing. But she'd always tell me that she was noth-ing but proud of me, and that I had not failed.

Going into college four years ago I didn't know what to expect. I didn't expect to get sicker, but I didn't expect it to be easy either. These years at the university have tested me mentally and physically, in ways I could have never imagined. To be a disabled twenty-two-year-old college student is not easy. I have good days and bad days. The most important aspect to have during these trying times is "patience and understanding" from my teachers and everyone else that I interacted with.

Sometimes it's a hassle dealing with me. I never ask for special treatment from teachers, only certain accommodations that comply with my disability. Every day is a challenge and just being able to get out of bed is a successful day in my book. I have always worked hard and will continue to work hard. My only goals right now are for me to get better and get my degree.

BRAIN RESEARCH AND LEARNING

Sierra's story may be difficult for some to read, but it is not uncommon that a school's population would be comprised of multiple students with a chronic illness. A chronic illness is a "medical condition . . . that lasts three months or more, affects a child's normal activities, and requires frequent hospitalizations, home health care, and/or extensive medical care" (Mokkink et al., 2008). Research findings estimate that 15.9 percent of children aged 6–11 and 17.5 percent of children 12–17 years old have at least one of eighteen chronic health conditions measured in the National Survey of Children's Health (NSCH, 2011/2012).

Thankfully, with medical advances and early detection methods, we are seeing children survive conditions that would have been considered life threatening in the past (Shiu). It is wonderful that advances in medicine have saved the lives of children. However, these advances also mean that more students will experience "short- and long-term cognitive, social, emotional, and behavioral difficulties that significantly interfere with their overall functioning" (Shiu, 2001, p. 269).

Research indicates that chronic illness often leads to higher absenteeism, cognitive impairments, or injuries from the condition, and various issues as a result of the medications used in the treatment process (Shaw et al., 2010). There is also growing evidence that argues that "chronic illnesses are related to impaired cognitive function in children and adolescents, either as a result of disease processes, aggressive forms of treatment, or both" (Compas, Jaser, Dunn, & Rodriguez, 2012, p. 465). Despite this growing body of research, little information exists on how to specifically assist students.

Additionally, each chronic illness presents its own cognitive issues. For example, if a child has early-onset type 1 diabetes there is likely to be "poor neuropsychological performance, with particular deficits in attention and executive function" (Compas et al., 2012, p. 467). Researchers have found "that the high levels of glucose in diabetic children can impede the formation of myelin and neurotransmitter regulation during critical stages of brain development" (Compas et al., 2012). Clearly, the varied chronic illnesses that may impact students will impact their cognitive abilities.

Other issues often arise for those who have been diagnosed with a chronic illness. As Sierra noted in her narrative, chronic illness often leads to increased absenteeism, anxiety, and depression (Shaw et al., 2010). These are common challenges for chronically ill students. In fact, in connection with absenteeism, many chronically ill students are more likely to repeat a grade (Lum, Wakefield, Donnan, Burns, Fardell, & Marshall, 2017).

However, in their meta-review of chronically ill students and their experiences in school, Lum et al. (2017) noted that when schools implemented "homebound education, school reintegration programs and individualized education plans" chronically ill students reported more positive school experiences (p. 43). In other words, when a school and its educators work to meet the needs of individual students, there are positive results.

When addressing the emotional needs of chronically ill students, it is important to understand that these students often experience high rates of anxiety and depression due to their conditions and isolation (Compas et al., 2012, Lum et al., 2017). Hinton and Kirk (2015) found that most teachers "lack the knowledge and confidence to meet pupils' medical, academic and social needs" because they were never trained to do so (p. 110). This is a clear deficiency that must be addressed.

This shortcoming is an important one because research indicates that when students are connected and engaged with their school they are more likely to be successful (Lum et al., 2017). Specifically, higher levels of engagement were linked to teachers who were supportive and positive when working with chronically ill students (Lum et al., 2017). To reach this level of support, teachers should coordinate with health-care professionals to learn the best methods required to meet the needs of chronically ill students.

CONCLUSION

This chapter highlights the experiences of Sierra, who was diagnosed with POTS, and research available regarding chronically ill students. The information presented in this chapter is applicable to students who suffer from other chronic illnesses as well. While there are many chronic illnesses and no systematic response, educators can become better equipped to work with chronically ill students through continued education, communication with students and their families, and collaboration with health-care specialists when needed.

READER TAKEAWAYS

- The unique academic and social needs of students with chronic illness must be taken into account.
- Educators have a duty and a responsibility to care for the whole student in order to teach the curriculum.
- Collaboration between a student's educators and their health-care providers can yield the best results for chronically ill students.

REFERENCES

Cox, E. R., Halloran, D. R., Homan, S. M., Welliver, S., & Mager, D. E. (2008). Trends in the prevalence of chronic medication use in children: 2002–2005. *Pediatrics, 122*, 1053–1061.

Compas, B. E., Jaser, S. S., Dunn, M. J., & Rodriguez, E. M. (2012). Coping with chronic illness in childhood and adolescence. *Annual Review of Clinical Psychology, 8*, 455–480.

Hinton, D., & Kirk, S. (2015) Teachers' perspectives of supporting pupils with long-term health conditions in mainstream schools: A narrative review of the literature. *Health & Social Care in the Community, 23*, 107–120.

Lum, A., Wakefield, C., Donnan, B., Burns, M., Fardell, J., & Marshall, G. (2017). Understanding the school experiences of children and adolescents with serious chronic illness: A systematic meta-review. *Child: Care, Health and Development, 43*(5), 645–662.

Mokkink L. B., van der Lee J. H., Grootenhuis M. A., Offringa M., & Heymans H. S. A. (2008). Defining chronic diseases and health conditions in childhood (ages 0–18 years of age): National consensus in the Netherlands. *European Journal of Pediatrics, 167*, 1441–1447.

National Survey of Children's Health. (NSCH, 2011/2012). *Data query from the child and adolescent health measurement initiative.* The Child & Adolescent Health Measurement Initiative. Retrieved from www.childhealthdata.org

Shaw, S. R., Glaser, S. E., Stern, M., Sferdenschi, C., & McCabe, P. C. (2010). Responding to students' chronic illnesses. *Principal Leadership, 10*(7), 12–16.

Shiu, S. (2001). Issues in the education of students with chronic illness. *International Journal of Disability, Development and Education, 48*(3), 269–281.

Thompson, R. J., & Gustafson, K. E. (1996). *Adaptation to chronic childhood illness.* Washington, DC: American Psychological Association.

Chapter 9

McKinney-Vento: "Choosing A or A": A Student Experiencing Homelessness

Donald M. Hume, PhD

The ache for home lives in all of us, the safe place where we can go as we are and not be questioned.

Maya Angelou

Expected Chapter Learning Outcomes:

- Readers will learn about the experience of a student with residential insecurity.
- Readers will learn how the stress of residential insecurity can affect students emotionally, socially, and academically.
- Readers will learn about ways to provide support to these students.

Earlier we looked at an example of a student who experienced residential instability through intake into the foster-care system (chapter 1). That student experienced frustration at the sudden inaccessibility of what was his: his clothes, his belongings, his family, and his house. What would it be like to not even have those things to miss?

Let's look at another example of a student with instability in her home life, but from another cause. Darla and her mother have been homeless since Darla was in the seventh grade. In what ways is Darla's reaction to her housing insecurity the same as that of the foster-care student from chapter 1? How is her reaction different? How might home insecurity manifest itself in classroom behavior and academic achievement?

STUDENT NARRATIVE

Darla: A Student Experiencing Homelessness

I was raised by two dads. When I was 13, I discovered that the reason we never spoke about my dad Dale's family, who lived in another state, is because they had disagreed with his lifestyle and disowned him. When my dad John was killed in a car accident during my seventh-grade year, I found out that his family, who had always seemed to accept us, also disagreed with their son's lifestyle. They no longer spoke to us and would not help pay for John's bills that were left behind.

Dale worked as a night-security guard at a local shopping mall and earned enough for us to be comfortable in a small apartment. That changed, however, when he was found on the floor of the security office one night. He was rushed to the hospital and was found to have suffered a stroke at the age of thirty-five.

He lost the ability to move his left leg, making him unable to continue as a security guard. He went on disability, but when the hospital bills began to arrive, those disability checks quickly proved meager. We owed way more than we could ever cover. Dale stopped going to his rehabilitation appointments in order to keep enough money for us to eat, but that meant that he wouldn't be able to go back to work, either.

We fell behind in rent by a couple of months and were evicted from our apartment. I remember that day, going through the things in my room trying to decide what to leave behind. There was only so much room in our car, and we had to leave room to sleep. In the end, I took just some clothes and a picture of me and John at the beach.

I didn't mind living out of the car. We'd usually try to find a parking lot of a big box store in a quieter part of town where we wouldn't be disturbed. A friend of my dad's gave him an extra key to the community pool in his neighborhood, and we'd go there two or three times a week to take a shower, early in the morning before anyone else would be there to see us.

I only missed school on days when Dale would get headaches so bad that he couldn't drive. Then I'd spend the day going back and forth from the car to the store where we had parked, walking the aisles to give him time to rest in quiet. I didn't have a way to contact my friends to find out what I missed, but I'd get the work from my teachers the next day and complete it that night, usually in a booth at a fast-food restaurant.

One night in the spring of my eighth-grade year, we were sleeping in the car as usual. Dale was stretched out as best he could in the back seat, and I was reclined in the front passenger seat, when we both were startled awake by a tapping on the window and flashlights in our eyes. It was the police. They told us we couldn't stay parked where we were because it was private property. They told us we could move the car out on the street, but it wouldn't start.

As the cops were calling a tow truck, I had to choose once more what items to take with me and which to leave behind, knowing we probably would never see the car again. There was just no money to get it fixed, so we knew it would get towed away and there was no way we could get it back. In addition to what I had on, I took one shirt, one pair of pants, and the picture of John.

I missed school for the next three days because the shelter where the cops dropped us off was on the other side of the county from my school. Eventually, we were able to call one of my friends from school, and her mom said we could stay with them until school got out.

It was nice having a bathroom and a shower where I was living. It's not something most people think of as a luxury, but when you have to plan using the restroom around store hours, suddenly having a bathroom seems like a dream come true. I also liked having a reliable place to do my homework. Despite living with my dad in our car for an entire year, my grades were still straight A's. I don't even think my teachers knew where I had been living.

That summer, Dale and I got kicked out of my friend's house. We were accused of taking advantage, of not appreciating the sacrifice of having us stay there. We didn't have a car to move back into, so Dale called one of John's friends who agreed to let us sleep on his couch and said he would come pick us up. He lived about eighty miles north which meant that I would have to start high school away from all of my friends in a new school district.

The school required proof of residency to enroll me, but, of course, we didn't have that. After Dale explained our situation, the school enrolled me right away. What I didn't know was that my school records would be emblazoned with the words "McKinney-Vento," announcing to all my teachers that I was a homeless student. (McKinney-Vento is the name of the federal Homeless Assistance Act which requires homeless students to be immediately enrolled in school, even without proof of residency in the attendance area.)

I enrolled in three honors courses my freshman year, and since we were staying with John's friend, I was able to have a regular place to do my reading and homework each night. I really didn't make new friends that year, which was probably a good thing since we got kicked out again about halfway through my freshman year. John's friend had a girlfriend move in with him, and we made the small accommodations too crowded and uncomfortable for her.

Dale phoned another of John's friends who said he could let us sleep in an attic room above the gas station he owned. There was no kitchen or furniture. At least we had access to a restroom, but without a shower. What else could we do? People talk about making choices in life, and express that in terms of options: "You can choose A or B." When you're homeless, though, you still *have to make choices, but the options are limited: "You can choose A or A, both of which suck." We waited on the curb for the gas station owner to pick us up.*

This friend lived another forty miles away, so I had to change schools in the middle of the year. Again, I was enrolled once we explained that we didn't have proof of residency, but this time I saw them write "McKinney-Vento" on my record.

Teachers at this school clearly weren't happy that I was enrolling in the middle of the year. Once my transfer grades arrived, though, and they saw that I did my work, even reading chapters from past units so I'd know what the rest of the class knew, things warmed up. Having my housing status announced on my records, though, did bother me. Not so much because my teachers knew I was homeless, but because they defined me by it.

One by one my teachers pulled me aside at some point during the remainder of that year to tell me how impressed they were. While I know they meant well in doing so, I don't think they realized how they were making me feel. Rather than just being impressed because I did well in school, they would begin their compliments by saying, "You've been through so much, but you still keep your grades up." Rather than seeing what I am, they wanted to focus on my circumstances, or least qualify what I am by those circumstances.

The worst thing was when they would assume I had a sensitivity because of my situation. I remember once we were watching a movie in Mrs. Fletcher's class, and she pulled me aside before class started to let me know there was a homeless person in the film and that it was okay if I wanted to go to the library instead of watch the film. "And remember, you can always talk to me," she said. I wanted to scream, "Why would I talk to you when you clearly don't know me?" Yes, I'm homeless. So are lots of people. It doesn't make me fragile.

Mrs. Luna was different. I remember one time I was having a bad day. I was worried that we were going to get kicked out of the garage because someone had discovered we were staying there overnight. I don't know what came over me, but I started to cry in the middle of class. This wasn't like me. I don't like to be emotional, so I just choose not to be. But here I was with tears streaming down my face. I got up and walked out of the room without asking permission, which was against the rules. I was gone for the rest of the period, but I came back into the room once it had emptied after class to collect my things. Mrs. Luna softly asked if I was okay. I told her I wasn't.

I explained what I was worried about, and she just let me. She didn't interrupt or try to hurry away. When I was done, she said, "I'm so sorry. I know there's nothing I can say that will make any of this better, and I won't pretend I can understand the kind of pressure you must be feeling." She wasn't trying to fix me or my situation. She just was letting me be me while letting me know that she cared.

This was important to me, because while I sometimes hated not having a shower every day, or sometimes a place to do my homework, I ultimately am glad that I have grown up the way I have. I know things that other students don't know, and it's all because of my experience being homeless. I appreciate things in a different way, even the little things. However, I don't want someone else's expectations or hang-ups pushed onto me and, this can make me build walls to protect myself even from people who think they're trying to help me. This can make it difficult for my peers and well-meaning teachers to understand me.

I sometimes have an edginess that other students don't have, but I think that's just because I've lost so much that I push people away trying to protect my emotions. It can be hard for me to be social, and I don't make friends very easily. When you have to expect that your whole life will be uprooted at a moment's notice every four to six months, you learn not to get too connected. Now that I'm about to graduate from high school, I have made some very close friends that I hope will stay with me forever, but in the back of my mind I'm not sure.

I don't need much from other people. My experience has taught me to fend for myself. I hated when teachers would assume that I need things I don't want or need. Mrs. Luna's approach, of just letting my experience be my experience, and giving me a place to be myself, was the most helpful thing any teacher has done for me.

BRAIN RESEARCH AND LEARNING

Both the foster student from chapter 1 and this homeless student, Darla, experience instability in their home lives. Matt's reaction was to reject the imposition of external structures until he himself opened to the idea and found a mentor he was willing to trust. Darla's reaction to home instability was to perform at high levels within the one stable structure she had in her life: school. For many students experiencing homelessness, school represents a stable and familiar environment that can soften the impact of instability at home (Benard, 1997).

Common stereotypes of what homelessness is can lead to presumptions that can interfere with our ability to identify students who need help. While sometimes irregular attendance can be an indicator of insecure housing (Ingram et al., 2017; Thielking, La Sala, & Flatau, 2017), often students experiencing homelessness are relatively well cared for, fed, with one or more parents actively involved in their education (Mohan & Shields, 2014). Homelessness by itself is not a form of neglect.

As teachers, we mustn't let our preconceived notions of what student needs look like interfere with our responsibility to personally engage with students to find out who they really are. Teachers are important adults in the lives of students and are well placed to be the first ones to notice early warning signs that signify a student is in need (Moore & McArthur, 2011).

One thing that can pull at a teacher's heartstrings is deciding whether a child who is experiencing homelessness is also being neglected. While this decision is difficult for individual teachers, even the U.S. government is unsure, stating that "it is unclear whether homelessness should be considered neglect" (DePanfilis, 2006, p. 12). No one doubts that residential instability has a multitude of negative effects on a child, but a parent's inability to provide consistent shelter may reflect a reality of poverty more than of parental neglect.

While the failure or inability to provide adequate shelter is included in most states' definitions of neglect, some states specifically omit homelessness *by itself* in their definitions of neglect. The key is in determining "adequate" shelter (and food, clothing, supervision, and medical treatment). Homelessness should be "considered neglect when the inability to provide shelter is the result of mismanagement of financial resources or when spending rent resources on drugs or alcohol results in frequent evictions" (Grayson & DePanfilis, 2000, p. 123).

Because so much of her life was out of her control, Darla wanted to exercise control over the small part of her life that she could. Unfortunately, her success at school initially hid her predicament from her teachers. While some students react the way the foster student from chapter 1 did, by ignoring his school work and other responsibilities, some, like Darla, will endeavor to persevere in their education despite unstable circumstances (Mohan & Shields, 2014). Even when she changed schools and was announced as homeless with the "McKinney-Vento" label, her high achievement indicated to her teachers that she may not need help.

The McKinney-Vento Homeless Assistance Act was originally signed by President Ronald Regan. It has been reauthorized several times since then. It provides certain rights to students who are experiencing homelessness, including the right to immediately enroll in the school where they present themselves.

According to this law, schools cannot segregate the homeless children from the general student population and must provide reasonable accommodations to ensure the student can fully participate in the curriculum. Districts are required to assign a liaison to assist with the retention of homeless students in the school system. Many schools will also indicate student enrollment in such a program in the student information system available to all teachers.

Darla herself did not feel that she wanted more connections at school. After initially suffering the loss of her parent, then the loss of her school and the friends she had there, her reaction was to limit her social interaction at school. Some students who experience the losses that often accompany homelessness will put up emotional barriers so they will not feel hurt in the future (Ahrens et al., 2011).

Mrs. Luna was able to break through this barrier in much the same way that Mr. Parker was able to do so with the foster student in chapter 1. An authentic interest in the student's emotional needs was the key that unlocked the relationship in both instances. Finding and keeping a personal connection with an adult at school can be an important way to minimize the isolation foster and homeless students often feel, and sometimes even seek (Moore & McArthur, 2011).

Even though they approached the issue of instability at home in very different ways, both Matt and Darla appreciated adult influence in their lives when they perceived that interest was authentic and rooted in a desire to know who they really were, without the adult presuming an understanding based upon assumptions about the student's circumstances.

CONCLUSION

Students need to feel safe and supported in order to achieve the growth and maturity that should be one of the products of schooling. Instability in housing or home life can interfere with feelings of safety, even in a stable environment like school. When students must choose between academic learning and concern about having their basic needs met, schooling can fall by the wayside (Brock, Louvar Reeves, & Nickerson, 2014). Teachers can be a powerful stabilizing force that can change a young person's life for the better immediately and for many years to come.

READER TAKEAWAYS

- Sometimes students' reaction to instability at home will be to value the stability they experience in school. These students will want to maintain high academic achievement despite whatever distractions exist in their home life. Often they can succeed in doing so, which can mask the needs they have.

- Students who experience residential insecurity want to be known for more than their circumstances. Praise the work they do, not the work "in spite of their circumstance."
- Assumptions about what a student experiencing homelessness needs, or what his or her situation demands, can lead to misguided attempts to show empathy. Engage with the student directly, and provide for the student's actual needs, rather than your assumptions.

REFERENCES

Ahrens, K. R., DuBois, D. L., Garrison, M., Spencer, R., Richardson, L. P., & Lozano, P. (2011). Qualitative exploration of relationships with important non-parental adults in the lives of youth in foster care. *Children and Youth Services Review, 33*(6), 1012–1023. doi:10.1016/j.childyouth.2011.01.006

Benard, B. (1997). Turning it around for all youth: From risk to resilience. ERIC/CUE Digest, Number 126.

Brock, S. E., Louvar Reeves, M. A., & Nickerson, A. B. (2014). Best practices in school crisis Intervention. In Patti L. Harrison and Alex Thomas (Eds.), *Best practices in school psychology* (pp. 211–230). Bethesda, MD: National Association of School Psychologists.

DePanfilis, D. (2006). *Child neglect: A guide for prevention, assessment, and intervention.* Washington, DC: U.S. Department of Health and Human Services.

Grayson, J., & DePanfilis, D. (2000). How do I determine if a child has been neglected? In H. Dubowitz & D. DePanfilis (Eds.), *Handbook for child protection practice* (pp. 121–126). Thousand Oaks, CA: Sage.

Ingram, E. S., Bridgeland, J. M., Reed, B., Atwell, M., Enterprises, C., & Associates, P. D. H. R. (2017). *Hidden in plain sight: Homeless students in America's public schools.* Washington, DC: Civic Enterprises.

Mohan, E., & Shields, C. M. (2014). The voices behind the numbers: understanding the experiences of homeless students. *Critical Questions in Education, 5*(3), 189–202.

Moore, T., & McArthur, M. (2011). "Good for kids": Children who have been homeless talk about school. *Australian Journal of Education, 55*(2), 147–160. doi:10.1177/000494411105500205

Thielking, M., La Sala, L., & Flatau, P. (2017). The role of teachers in identifying and supporting homeless secondary school students: Important lessons for teacher education. *Australian Journal of Teacher Education, 42*(8), 95–109.

Chapter 10

When Normal Is Not Normal

Heather Dean, PhD

No significant learning can occur without a significant relationship.

James Comer

Expected Chapter Learning Outcomes:

- Readers will gain insight into the experiences of a high school student from a stable home environment that encountered trauma during her senior year.
- Readers will be provided with brain research that connects to experiences of the student highlighted in this chapter.

The danger in a text like this is educators might have the tendency to overlook the needs of the students that appear to have every advantage. Children who come from a stable home with married and gainfully employed parents who are involved in their education still endure hardship, loss, and struggle.

As educators strive to meet the needs of the at-risk students discussed in the prior chapters of this book, please don't forget that each student in classes from the coast of California to the mountains of Tennessee to the white sandy beaches of Florida arrive at school each day with very real needs deserving of care.

Consider the story that follows, recounted by a young woman reminiscing about a difficult time in her high school years. Would teachers have recognized any changes in her behavior or personality? In what ways must educators remember that each student counts and deserves care and attention?

STUDENT NARRATIVE

Hand in Hand

My grandmother and I have the same handwriting. Big dancing G's and noisy boisterous D's. Our letters curl like smoke, inhabiting huge portions of lines, camping out across the frontier of every page.

I remember when we first discovered our doppelganger handwriting. I had hastily scribbled out some sort of note for my parents and left it on the kitchen counter for them to find when my grandmother ambled in, followed by the acrid scent of her cigarettes and two massively overweight pugs.

She was looking in the cupboard for a mid-afternoon post-smoke snack when she saw my note lying on the counter. She eyed it for a second, confused.

"I didn't write this," she mumbled, wondering whose hand had rubbed slightly over the last words, smearing the ink. She looked up at me.

"Who wrote this?"

"I did."

She gazed at me, and her face broke into one of my favorite yellow-toothed smiles.

"It's just like mine."

I don't know how I had never noticed before, but she was right. Our handwriting was nearly indistinguishable.

I was so happy. I wanted to roll in ink and be one of the spiraling letters we each could spin onto the page. I loved this random meaningless, meaningful connection between me and my grandmother.

You see, my grandmother had always been my favorite person. When I was four years old, I would sit beside her, me in my little red rocking chair and her in a big marshmallowy recliner. QVC would be playing on the elephantine TV in front of us, hawking gaudy jewelry or extravagant lotions.

Her pug, Pearl, would always be curled up in her lap, like a living snorting heating pad, and we would always each have a cup of coffee in hand. Mine was more than likely 90 percent French vanilla creamer, but at the time it felt very adult.

Often, my grandmother would look at me and ask, "Well, should we get it, Grace?" And I knew the correct answer was always yes. Do it. My high-pitched four-year-old voice encouraging her as she reached for the phone. When the call was over, she would hit the 'end' button like an Olympian climbing to the top of the podium. She would look at me with this gold medal glint in her eye, thrilled for what next week's mail would bring.

And it makes sense that we would have similar handwriting; we are such similar people. Handwriting psychologists say that people like me and my grandmother who write such large, filling letters tend to be more outgoing, people-oriented, and life of the party types. This is entirely true of my grandmother.

I remember as a young girl overhearing my mom, my aunt, and my grandmother discussing a man she had met on a plane. His name was Max ("Max-a-million" they joked), and after sitting beside my grandma on a flight back to California, he asked her on a date. They went on a few dates, and ultimately nothing came of it, but even in her fifties, my grandmother was still charming people.

While I was in high school, she worked in a smoke shop. She was the type of clerk customers loved, someone who could relate to them, laugh with them, and make them feel at home even as they bought their Camels and Marlboros. The few times I went to see her there, the customers would be so excited to meet me. Wow, Joan's granddaughter! I was a novelty, because I was hers.

She lit up every room like a chandelier, dazzling everyone with her good humor and charm, making them feel more beautiful. She was perfect. Flawless. Unencumbered by the defects that weigh the rest of us down.

But handwriting psychologists also say that people who write like me and my grandmother tend to put up a front and hide their true emotions. By the time the shoes were scattered across the floor this was clear. By the time the microwave had been hurled to the ground, by the time the yelling started, by the time the hollow vodka bottles clanging in her trash could no longer be muffled, it all became clear.

I remember that day, October 7, 2014, in such a vivid, un-erasable way that not even Mr. Clean himself could scrub it away. I was a senior in high school, preparing for the Homecoming Dance in a mere four days, ecstatic about the boy who had asked me. It was early in the evening, maybe about six o'clock, when the yelling began.

I was sitting on the floor of my bedroom, which was decorated with the brightest orange paint your eyes have ever seen, doing homework. There was no warning, no escalation, no preamble to what happened next. It was just silent one minute, and then the world was awake with screaming, right outside my bedroom door.

My grandmother, my beloved, perfect grandmother, was on the other side of my door yelling obscene, vicious things at my parents. I sat stock still listening to every word, each like prongs in a shredder, annihilating my perception of my grandma.

Minutes strolled by like hours, as she throttled my parents with insults, each one seeming to fuel her desire to spit out the next, each one landing on my ears like jabs and hooks and uppercuts. She would not be out-boxed.

Soon she brought the battle to my room, trying to drag me into it. I remember her face, wearing a manic expression I had never seen before, pleading with me to agree with her. Isn't your dad an asshole? Don't they treat me poorly? You see, right Grace?

My dad put himself between us, finally raising his voice, finally entering the ring. *Get away from her! Get away from her!* Her wrath now returned to him in full force, but he was able to close my door, protecting me. For the first time since this began, I stood up. I shakily turned the lock on my door, holing myself in. Waiting out the storm.

I later found out that my brothers in this moment were doing the same thing. They had locked themselves in their room, and Johnny, brave enough to do what I wasn't, called the police. At some point, before they arrived, my grandmother retreated to her room, and my parents hurriedly gathered us up before she could start in on round two.

Leaving my room, and heading for the door, I had only a few moments to take in the carnage of my home. Bright blue sneakers and worn flip-flops were scattered on the floor. Kitchen drawers hung open, their contents sprinkled across the tile. The microwave now on the hall carpet.

I wanted desperately for this all to be a lie, a trick. I wanted someone to wave a wand and silverware to magically fly back to its drawer, shoes to return to the bin, and everything fall right back into place. I wanted my grandmother to come out and be smiling and take a bow alongside my parents. I wanted it all to be a show, a performance, anything but reality.

We all piled into our Honda Odyssey and drove away. A few hours later, we came back to hastily pack our bags. My grandmother screamed at me as I ran out to my car. *Hey, you're going to ignore your grandmother? You're going to run away from your grandma?* My brother defended me, yelling back at her, drawing her away from me.

My dad attempted to drive away in his truck, only to realize that in our absence my grandmother had slashed all four of his tires. My brothers piled into my car, and with barely a glance back I drove off. Eventually my parents followed, towing bags of miscellaneous belongings, and drove to the local Holiday Inn.

We lived in the Holiday Inn for three days. The police removed my grandmother from our home so we could go back and pack up the rest of our belongings. On Saturday, October 11, 2014, members of our church came and helped us move all our furniture, finish packing, and move our things to a friend's house.

My parents insisted I still go to Homecoming. So, while everyone else was filling musty cardboard boxes and hauling the remnants of our life with our grandmother away, I was sitting in front of my mirror, carefully applying eyeliner and blush; painting my face, painting on happiness and excitement. I slipped into the black dress my mother and I had picked out and slid my feet into maroon Comfort Plus+ heels.

My date picked me up at an empty house, devoid of furniture and any signs of life. He slid the corsage onto my wrist, and we left. I had an incredible *time. We had burgers for dinner, danced all night, and got Baja Blast Freezes from Taco Bell afterwards. I was happy. Surprisingly, happy. This was an escape. I drove to our family friend's house that night, and drifted asleep on an air mattress, too tired to take off my makeup, too happy not to have sweet dreams.*

Over the course of the next week, we would find a house available for rent in our school district and move everything once again. My senior year continued just the same, except without the presence of my grandmother. I was now putting up a front too. I am happy. I am not broken. I am a people-person, a people-pleaser, the ever un-phased Grace Thompson.

It seems silly that watching my grandmother's façade crumble, caused me to build my own. If I had learned anything from this experience it should have been that the walls we build do not last; they cannot stand. As they begin to fall, the people around us start to get glimpses in. On tiptoes they stand, trying to peer over, until finally the bricks are dismantled, the concrete thunderously destroyed, and we are seen in all our gruesome glory.

My grandmother had been hiding behind her walls for so long, that sometimes I feel like I never even really knew her. After the walls fell, my mom revealed to me what her and my father had tried to shelter me from for so long.

My grandmother grew up in an abusive home, hiding in a dog house from her father's alcohol fueled fists. She became pregnant at seventeen, and was given up by her parents. She numbed all this with family packs of cigarettes, liters of Blue Sky vodka, and copious amounts of marijuana. She battled depression and bipolar disorder her whole life.

And we have the same handwriting.

Ever since these events that have permanently changed me, I have worried that this connection between my grandmother and I that I once reveled in, is an omen. A sign of my own future. This person, who more than anything I wanted to become, I am afraid of becoming.

I have not spoken to my grandmother since October 7, 2014. But she is still present in my mind and in my heart like an artery. I have realized my own path is already vastly different than the one she had set out on when she was twenty. I have realized I do not have to be her. Yet, I still look down at every letter I write, and see her wrapped up in them. I look at every letter I write, and see her.

BRAIN RESEARCH AND LEARNING

Despite the hardship this student encountered, she maintained straight A's, remained active in sports and leadership at her high school, and participated in a healthy social life. Fortunately for Grace, she had advantages others did not, with the support of her parents and siblings. Nevertheless, her experience with trauma had an impact on her year, her ability to sleep as well as on her cognitive functioning.

Dr. John Medina, a developmental molecular biologist, notes that "a stable, positive social environment in the home change how children regulate their stress hormone systems, and stress hormone regulation has a direct effect on executive function development. . . . Kids in relationally safe homes have more robust executive function ability because they consistently experience lower stress hormone levels" (2018).

Brain research continues to demonstrate that students that encounter acute stress, as that described by Grace, will be unable to process information as effectively as they do in times void of stress. David Sousa, an international consultant in educational neuroscience, explains, "There is a hierarchy of response to sensory input. Any input that is of higher priority diminishes the processing of data of lower priority. The brain's main job is to help its owner survive. Thus, it will process immediately any data interpreted as posing a threat to the survival of the individual. . . . Upon receiving the stimulus, the reticular activating system sends a rush of adrenaline throughout the brain. This reflexive response shuts down all unnecessary activity and directs the brain's attention to the source of the stimulus" (2017).

Eric Jensen agrees. He writes, "Stress adversely affects cognition. . . . Exposure to chronic or acute stress is debilitating. The most common adaptive behaviors include increased anxiety and an increased sense of detachment or helplessness" (Jensen, 2010).

Often, educators, counselors, and those working in social services share that student misbehaviors are frequently an indicator of some type of trauma or unmet need. Educators and others dealing with youth need to be cognizant of changes in behavior, grades, or personality. Sousa advocates for teachers to understand their power and potential within their classroom. "Teachers can . . . promote emotional security in the classroom by establishing a positive climate that encourages students to take appropriate risks" (2017).

According to Zaretta Hammond, "The brain's two prime directives are to stay safe and be happy. . . . We cannot downplay students' need to feel safe and valued in the classroom. . . . It is not enough to have a classroom free of psychological and social threats. The brain needs to be part of a caring social community to maximize its sense of well-being" (2015).

CONCLUSION

Today's teachers are more aware of the impact of life experiences on the student's ability to learn and process new information. Recently, a new term, *pedagogy of care*, has been introduced within education circles. Carol Murray defines pedagogy of care as a science.

Murray writes, "Now more than ever, we possess the brain research that demonstrates what we've always known instinctively: children are learning from the moment they are born and the most meaningful lessons are embedded in care. Nothing drives learning as powerfully as eye contact, touch, and voice—the essential elements in the pedagogy of care" (Murray, 2016).

As educators strive to meet the needs of various learners, they must also remember the ways they greet and interact with students daily often make an impact, even if that impact might remain seemingly invisible.

This text was designed to give educators and other professions that serve students a peek into the varied lives of students. Teachers, with the endless lesson planning, grading, and classroom management, are easily prone to neglecting one of the most powerful and essential components to being an effective and impactful teacher building relationships.

Please remember that all students have their own story and that all of them are deserving of attention. While no teacher can meet all students' needs, each educator certainly can make a difference to some. With that concept in mind, please enjoy the following story by Loren Eiseley.

The Starfish Story

While walking along a beach, an elderly gentleman saw someone in the distance leaning down, picking something up and throwing it into the ocean.

As he got closer, he noticed that the figure was that of a young man, picking up starfish one by one and tossing each one gently back into the water.

He came closer still and called out, "Good morning! May I ask what it is that you are doing?"

The young man paused, looked up, and replied, "Throwing starfish into the ocean."

The old man smiled, and said, "I must ask, then, why are you throwing starfish into the ocean?"

To this, the young man replied, "The sun is up and the tide is going out. If I don't throw them in, they'll die."

Upon hearing this, the elderly observer commented, "But, young man, do you not realize that there are miles and miles of beach and there are starfish all along every mile? You can't possibly make a difference!"

The young man listened politely. Then he bent down, picked up another starfish, threw it back into the ocean past the breaking waves, and said, "It made a difference for that one."

READER TAKEAWAYS

- *All* students are worthy of our attention and in need of our care.
- Brain research confirms that students are unable to learn effectively when they do not feel safe.
- Educators have a duty and a responsibility to care for the whole child in order to teach the curriculum.

REFERENCES

Eiseley, L. C. (1979). *The star thrower.* New York, NY: Harcourt Brace Jovanovich.

Hammond, Z., & Jackson, Y. (2015). *Culturally responsive teaching and the brain: Promoting authentic engagement and rigor among culturally and linguistically diverse students.* Thousand Oaks, CA: Corwin.

Jensen, E. (2010). *Teaching with poverty in mind: What being poor does to kids brains and what schools can do about it.* Alexandria, VA: Association for Supervision and Curriculum Development.

Medina, J. (2018). *Attack of the teenage brain!: Understanding and supporting the weird and wonderful adolescent learner.* Alexandria, VA: Association for Supervision and Curriculum Development.

Murray, C. (2016, August 2). *What is the pedagogy of care?* Retrieved from http://www.communityplaythings.com/resources/articles/2016/the-pedagogy-of-care

Sousa, D. A. (2017). *How the brain learns.* Thousand Oaks, CA: Corwin.

About the Authors

Heather Dean, PhD, has spent her career in education teaching English at the junior high and high school levels. Currently, she is an assistant professor of teacher education at California State University, Stanislaus. Her research interests include teacher retention, literacy education, as well as understanding the best practices for training new teachers.

Donald Hume, PhD, has more than eighteen years of experience in teaching secondary English. He also teaches courses in curriculum, instruction, assessment, and classroom management in the credential program at California State University, Long Beach.

Heidi C. Kuehn has been teaching social science and German at a comprehensive public high school for the past twenty-five years. Driven by an interest in diversity and inclusivity in education, Heidi is currently finishing her doctoral studies on transgender students' high school experiences at California Lutheran University. In the future, the lifelong educator plans to work with undergraduate and graduate students in education and hopes to continue her work with schools' professional development programs.

Dana Mayhall, PhD, is currently an assistant professor of teacher education at Abilene Christian University in Abilene, Texas. She has more than twenty years of experience serving as teacher and administrator in elementary and secondary education, and more than ten years of experience in teacher education. She works with teacher candidates in their school placements as well as providing instruction in educational foundations and methods, multicultural perspectives and culturally relevant pedagogy, and reframing learning at the graduate level.

Jon McFarland, EdD, has been an educator for over two decades and has worked at multiple levels in public and private education. Currently, he is an assistant professor of teacher education. His research interests include the utilization of gamification in academic settings, issues of student motivation and engagement, effective uses of educational technology, and matters of equity and diversity in secondary schools.

Derek Riddle, PhD, has taught secondary English and has had experiences in teaching at all grade levels (7–12), remedial to advanced students, and in both urban and rural areas for about ten years. Currently, he is an assistant professor of teacher education at California State University, Stanislaus. His research interests include teacher professional development, co-teaching, English education, literacy education, and teacher recruitment and retention.

Jennifer Rumsey, PhD, has been a public school educator for twenty years. She has taught reading and English to students in grades 6–11, served as English Department Chair on two campuses, and is currently a middle school counselor. A mother of two children with attention-deficit/hyperactivity disorder (ADHD), Jennifer has researched and read extensively about ADHD, and she works to inform educators about best practices in serving children with this disability.

Amber E. Wagnon, PhD, was a public school secondary educator for over a decade. Currently, she is an assistant professor of secondary education at Stephen F. Austin State University, where her research interests include literacy education, experiential learning, and public school advocacy.

Natalie Welcome, PhD, currently serves as an instructor of mathematics at Arizona State University, College of Integrated Sciences and Arts. She works closely with many first- and second-year college students in need of math content remediation and/or disability support, helping them overcome challenges that can inhibit degree completion. Her primary courses taught include college algebra, precalculus, and calculus for life sciences. In addition, she directs a study-abroad program that leads students to study the history of mathematics in various parts of the world.